The War Within

The War Within

Israel's Ultra-Orthodox Threat to Democracy and the Nation

YUVAL ELIZUR AND
LAWRENCE MALKIN

OVERLOOK DUCKWORTH
NEW YORK • LONDON

This edition first published in hardcover in the United States and the United
Kingdom in 2013 by Overlook Duckworth, Peter Mayer Publishers, Inc.

NEW YORK
141 Wooster Street
New York, NY 10012
www.overlookpress.com
For bulk and special sales, please contact sales@overlookny.com

LONDON
90-93 Cowcross Street
London EC1M 6BF
info@duckworth-publishers.co.uk
www.ducknet.co.uk

Cataloging-in-Publication Data is available from the Library of Congress

Book design and typeformatting by Bernard Schleifer
Manufactured in the United States of America
ISBN US: 978-1-4683-0345-2
ISBN UK: 978-0-7156-4519-2

To the memory of Judith Elizur
So devoted to religious freedom and women's rights

Contents

The War Within

An Anxious Call

LATE ONE WINTRY EVENING THE TELEPHONE RANG ON MY desk in Jerusalem. A man's voice at the other end of the line spoke softly in Hebrew without any distinguishing accent. He sounded like a man in the prime of life. "I want you to help me," he pleaded, almost without emotion. He identified himself as a member of a religious seminary and did not wait for a reply.

"I have a wife and five children. All day I study Talmud. I get a living allowance of eleven hundred shekels [about $300] a month as well as a stipend to cover my tuition. I also receive government welfare payments for the children and some help from friends abroad. In the mornings, my wife helps in a dress shop. Altogether we have about thirty-five hundred shekels [about $900] a month to live on. We have no apartment of our own, and our parents are willing to help us buy one, but who can afford to buy an apartment these days?"

No doubt he had heard of, or perhaps had actually read, the earlier version of this book that was published in Hebrew in 2009, so it only seemed right to cut into his sadly familiar tale.

"Why do you stay in the yeshiva? Why don't you look for a job?"

"What job?" he angrily replied. "What can I do? In Talmud Torah [primary school] I was never taught mathematics, English, or even Hebrew grammar. I wanted to become an accountant, but I am not qualified . . ."

"Why don't you take evening courses?" I countered.

The emotion that was lacking before now shone through. "How can I? In the evenings I have to help my wife and children at home. If I take courses, everyone in the yeshiva will criticize me. My rabbi says one must study only holy subjects. I am not a hero."

"So what do you want me to do?" I was about to end the conversation.

"You can help. You are a writer. Don't let this madness continue. This country needs thousands of workers. Don't let the politicians ruin our lives."

"But what good will our writing do?" I argued. "The vote of your representatives in the Knesset is needed to uphold the government coalition. That is more important to them than your happiness."

"So why don't they select only the best and the brightest to maintain and propagate the study of Jewish wisdom, as they did in Europe before the Holocaust? Do they really need ninety thousand yeshiva students to keep Jewish learning going? They have far fewer scientists in the Weitzman Institute and research persons in our high-tech industry and look at our achievements!"

I was slow in replying, and he continued, raising his voice: "I'll tell you why. They are afraid that I and thousands like me will serve in the army, associate with other Israelis, find good jobs, and gradually leave their flock. They are not concerned about my soul. They are worried about their jobs."

"But what will my writing do?" I tried to appeal to his logic, but he became even more emotional: "You already did very much!

Why do you think the Supreme Court tore up the Tal Law that gave the *haredim* an excuse not to serve in the army? The leaders of the religious parties miscalculated. They believed the Israeli public will swallow everything, including the separation of women on public buses."

He continued: "Our leadership was given another blow by the government that has recently decided to raise the minimum legal age of marriage from seventeen to eighteen. Israeli society does not want our children to get married before they have a mind of their own and immediately have millions of children whom they cannot support and become more dependent on the budgets the leaders can obtain for them."

And then, just as I thought the conversation had come to an end, he added: "We are in for a very interesting period. A period of a war within. Until recently the secular forces made all the mistakes. Recently my people have begun making mistakes. That is good. That will save Israel."

—Yuval Elizur

1

Jerusalem:
A Divided Capital

As you approach Meah She'arim, the trees begin to disappear. In Zichron Moshe and Geula you will still find a few bare trees, and at the rear of the houses grass still grows in the winter. But in the alleys that surround Meah She'arim, in the blocks of nearby houses, and in Meah She'arim itself, there is neither a tree nor a bush. No grass pushes up between the cobblestones. Even the plants so typical of Jerusalem's stone walls cannot be found here. It is a landscape without earth, a world without the color green. Not even a flowerpot can be seen, only stone walls, cement blocks, galvanized or rusty metal sheets. A mixture of railings, barred windows, clotheslines heavy with white laundry: a gray world of brown, white and black mixed with the black, gray and striped color of the clothes and above all the psychedelic colors of the advertisements. The yellow and pink letters call from the walls. But there are no birds chirping.

—*Ariel Hirschfeld*, literary critic, quoted in
"The Haredi Community and Environmental Quality"

MORE THAN ANYWHERE ELSE IN THE WORLD, JERUSALEM IS a city of living history. On the Sabbath—or really any day of the week—one can see phalanxes of ultra-Orthodox believers making their way to the Western Wall undisturbed in the fur hats, long sidecurls, and black garb of the Jewish ghettos of Eastern Europe that were destroyed in the Holocaust. Some visitors find their quaint appearance reassuring as a sign of the toughness of Jewish tradition in reviving the vanished life of the Eastern European shtetl. Others are appalled by their almost ghostly revival in modern Israel, bursting out of their once-cloistered life of study and prayer in the city's neighborhood known as Meah She'arim, or One Hundred Gates. The ultra-Orthodox haredim—

literally "those who tremble" (in awe of God)—depend on the largesse of the State of Israel while refusing to recognize its law until the day the Messiah arrives. It is as if they have declared: "We are not part of the Zionist state; we just happen to live here."

For nineteen years, between 1948 and 1967, Meah She'arim was not only part of Israel's ideological fringe but the actual border between the Jewish state and the part of Palestine ruled by the Kingdom of Jordan. The Mandelbaum Gate, named after a lonely building on the outskirts of the ultra-Orthodox community, was the only place where diplomats and tourists could legally pass between the two states. No goods were allowed to cross at all except for an official exchange of daily newspapers. In some respects Jerusalem remained divided even after the 1967 victory, not only between Jews and Arabs but between the ultra-Orthodox Jews and all others.

Until recently it looked as if the spread of the ultra-Orthodox was gaining momentum. They penetrated secular neighborhoods as young families moved away from the nation's capital to escape what they viewed as a medieval cage. In several other neighborhoods, Orthodox inhabitants displaced secular families attracted by the opportunities of technical and professional employment in the business and industrial centers along the coastal plain. By 2012 about one-third of Jerusalem's Jewish population was haredim, triple their proportion of Israel's Jewish population of about six million.

In 1967, Jerusalem's Jewish inhabitants numbered fewer than four hundred thousand. Since then the city's population has almost tripled. Not only have Jewish immigrants poured into the city from all corners of the world, but the number of Muslims has risen significantly through natural growth and the attraction of better-paid jobs for Arabs from Israel, the West Bank, and Jordan. While complaining—often justifiably—of discrimination in

On the third day of the Six-Day War in 1967, Israeli paratroopers entered the walled Old City of Jerusalem, which had been in Jordanian hands for nearly two decades, and stood in awe of the Western Wall, the holiest site in Jewish tradition. These s ecular soldiers had fought all night to conquer the city and taken heavy casualties. This celebrated photo, taken by David Rubinger of Time magazine, became a symbol of reverence by all Jews and not just the ultra-Orthodox haredim.

obtaining building permits and budgets for education, garbage collection, and other municipal services, Jerusalem's Arab population has been augmented by construction workers, garbage collectors, policemen, and taxi drivers. Arab doctors and nurses work in Jerusalem's Hadassah and Sha'areri Tzedek hospitals as well in the health insurance clinics. Only Christian Jerusalemites were emigrating, mostly to overseas countries.

Jewish Jerusalem has also changed demographically since 1967. While Jewish immigrants poured into the capital and often found employment in the city's government offices, academic institutions, and high-tech industries, there was an even more pronounced influx of ultra-Orthodox—not only to the somewhat slum-like neighborhoods of Meah She'arim, Geulah, and Mekor Baruch, but to attractive new haredi communities that sprang up mainly in the north and east of the city.

Many described this process as an Orthodox invasion, even a deliberate attempt to change the way of life in the city. Secular Jerusalemites feared their city was becoming a religious stronghold where cars would not move on the Sabbath and restaurants would close tight, and on the holy day of rest no radio and television could be heard through open windows—only the chanting of the traditional prayers from the multitude of synagogues. Everyone in Jerusalem remembers the ceremony inaugurating an imposing new bridge at the entrance of the city, designed by Santiago Calatrava, to serve the newly built light railway (which runs only six days a week). The then-ruling haredi mayor, Uri Lupolyansky, made the girls in the dance group amend their costumes to cover their arms and legs in the name of "modesty." Far more disturbing was the diversion of most of the municipal housing budget to haredi families demanding priority because they had more children.

Laundry lines "decorating" the main streets of Meah She'arim, one of the main enclaves of Jersualem's ultra-Orthodox community

If the haredim had their way, all Jewish Jerusalem would be shut down on the Sabbath. As it is, restaurants seeking kosher certification are forbidden to open for business on Friday nights and on Saturday. Still, more and more places of entertainment in non-Orthodox neighborhoods find it possible to provide food and entertainment on the Sabbath even though it is not kosher. This relaxation of strict regulation is accompanied by a push by city officials to entice young couples to move back to Jerusalem, and there are indications that the migration to the economically vibrant coastal communities has recently slowed or even stopped. Osnat Kollek, the daughter of the legendary mayor Teddy Kollek, who governed the city for more than thirty years, recently returned after living in self-imposed exile on the coast for eighteen years. "I was afraid to expose my three children to an atmosphere of intolerance and extreme religiosity," she said, "but I realized what I missed by not living in Jerusalem. Even before I left there was a rich cultural life here, concerts, lectures, and even fine restaurants open on Shabbat, or the Sabbath. Today there are many more young people, students, artists, and numerous volunteers who strive to improve life in Jerusalem." The city's renowned Israel Museum attracted 1.4 million visitors after an expansion and modernization program was completed in 2010. Several Reform and Conservative synagogues have been established in Jerusalem; these American-based non-Orthodox institutions conduct seminars to train rabbis and scholars. There is even a pluralistic religious group involved with municipal politics, with Councilwoman Rachel Azaria well known for her ability to defuse religious disputes.

But all these signs of liberalization do not change the fact that clashes between the secular majority and the ultra-Orthodox minority in Jerusalem are the fiercest and most violent in the entire State of Israel. It was here that fundamentalist Jewish orthodoxy was transformed from a cultural and spiritual minority into a political force pressing its religious claims in a way that threatens the stability of the nation and could affect its future. Deploying the bloc votes of their followers to take advantage of a system of proportional representation that ensures parliamentary seats for all but the tiniest minority parties, the haredim have long exploited their balancing power in the Knesset. No coalition government has been able to survive without the support of the handful of members from the religious parties. But rather than acting as kingmakers, their leaders have chosen to exact concessions for parliamentary support of their increasingly separate society that ironically declines to answer to its elected leaders and only follows its rabbis.

Ultra-Orthodox eighteen-year-olds have been exempt from compulsory military service, unlike all other Israeli Jews, men and women. The intensifying pressure from the military, which needs more combat troops, and the courts, which view the dispute as a matter of equality before the law, has built slowly toward political crisis. A resolution seemed imminent when Prime Minister Benjamin Netanyahu formed a parliamentary coalition in the spring of 2012 with the twenty-seven Knesset members of the center-right Kadima Party led by a retired commander of the Israel Defense Forces—the IDF—Shaul Mofaz. A principal goal of this political maneuvering was to use their combined majority of an overwhelming 94 parliamentary votes out of 120 to enact a law that would have brought ultra-Orthodox youngsters into the army. But almost as quickly as the coalition came together, Netanyahu yielded to pressure from Orthodox politicians, reinforced by public prayers against the law led by ultra-Orthodox rabbis. Kadima quit the coalition, leaving the issue to further polarize Israeli society.

Only 17 percent of haredi young men answered the national call to arms in 2011 compared to three-quarters of other Jewish eighteen-year-old men who were conscripted. Another 14 percent of the ultra-Orthodox accepted civilian service as well as 8 percent of Arab Israelis, mainly young women teachers, a new factor in the debate over restoring a universal draft.

Many other issues divide the haredim from Israel's predominantly secular society, and they are likely to continue to fester, however durable any compromise over military service proves to be. The state provides full financial support for their ultras' religious yeshivot—the Hebrew plural for a seminary known as a yeshiva. Mathematics, English, and science are not taught in these seminaries nor even in ultra-Orthodox elementary schools, leaving graduates unemployable in a modern economy. Only 3 percent are literate in English. Many continue to pursue religious studies, and those who do are subsidized up to the age of forty and above. Their devotion to biblical law strengthens the dominance of Orthodox rabbis, the only kind permitted to preside at state-supported religious services in Israel. These rabbis control marriage, divorce, and matters ranging from the food sold throughout the nation to the truncated Sabbath schedule of the national airline. Immigrants seeking citizenship under Israel's Law of Return who have not already converted abroad must satisfy Orthodox religious tests to be officially recognized as Jews in Israel, straining the founding ideal of the place as a homeland for all Jews.

When their demands are not met in full, the ultra-Orthodox routinely threaten to bring down the government with the help of their political allies or even without them. In 1968 they joined with the religious Zionist parties and resigned from Yitzhak Rabin's first government, forcing early elections. Their complaint: a squadron of Phantom fighters, the first warplanes to be supplied by the United States, landed in Israel on a Friday evening close to sundown but was nevertheless received at an official celebration. Because the religious parties insist biblical law must take precedence over any constitution, or indeed all matters of state, Israel has been prevented from adopting a formal founding document despite the commitment of Israel's founding fathers in the Declaration of Independence proclaimed on May 15, 1948.

Since that time the ultra-Orthodox have been allowed to fashion a privileged community that enfolds, protects, and isolates its adherents in a bizarre culture with a cloistered and often strangely skewed view of the world. For example, as the political negotiations over the obligation of military service intensified, three haredi men were arrested in connection with spray-painted graffiti on the Yad Vashem Holocaust memorial and similar messages scrawled around Jerusalem's Warsaw Ghetto Square. They read: THE ZIONISTS WANTED THE HOLOCAUST and IF HITLER HAD NOT EXISTED, THE ZIONISTS WOULD HAVE INVENTED HIM.

Only in 2010 had the first hints of resistance to the haredim's extraordinary veto power over vast areas of secular life begun to appear in the courts and in civic action against the government. This secular backlash has been intensified by fears engendered by the extraordinary growth of the haredim. The Central Bureau of Statistics estimated that at the end of 2009, approximately six hundred thousand Israelis belonged to ultra-Orthodox communities, or about 10 percent of Israel's Jewish population. Their numbers are growing rapidly, as well as their share of the population, mainly because their birthrate of 7.7 children per family is twice that of the Israeli Jewish average. Registration for the 2013 school year indicates that for the first time in Israel's history, the number of six-year-olds in Orthodox and religious schools will exceed the number of secular students.

But the share of the ultra-Orthodox men in the labor force has until recently been the lowest in the developed world: 65 percent between the ages of thirty-five and fifty-five are not gainfully employed, or more than five times the average male unemployment rate in the same age group in Western societies.

These figures far exceed the statistics describing their Jewish coreligionists in all other advanced countries, where they must support themselves and their families without disproportionate government support. Paradoxically, the Diaspora haredim are closer to Jewish tradition in their search for employment and business ventures to support their observant and studious lives than the ultra-Orthodox in Israel, despite their claim to be bringing the old ways back to life. In fact, never in Jewish history has such a large proportion of the male Jewish community devoted itself exclusively to religious studies: of the ten million Jews in Europe before World War II, the number of full-time religious seminarians averaged only about four thousand.

But in Israel, these perpetual religious seminary students are encouraged to spend their days in study and prayer by government stipends and foreign charities. A higher proportion of ultra-Orthodox women work to help support their large families, although mainly at subsistence level. In 2008, government statistics show that more than 60 percent of ultra-Orthodox families lived below the poverty level, against 12 percent of other Jewish families in Israel. The real income of the haredim may be somewhat higher, however, because they tend to hide earnings from what they call the "evil eyes" of the tax authorities.

In the major cities of Tel Aviv, Haifa, and Jerusalem the majority of taxpayers are not haredim, and the taxes paid by the secular majority cover the costs of the municipal services for the total population. But in haredi-majority towns, the municipalities depend on generous subsidies from the Interior Ministry. Netivot, a town with an Orthodox majority, receives an annual subsidy from the central government of 30 million shekels, or about $8 million, to provide civic services for a population of about twenty-six thousand. Carmiel, a mostly secular town in the Galilee with a population almost twice that of Netivot, qualifies for a central government grant of only five million shekels. This gross disparity can be accounted for by the fact that in recent years the minister of the interior has been a member of the ultra-Orthodox Shas Party; in this case, the strength of his political leverage can be literally counted in cash.

WHAT EXPLAINS THE ENORMOUS POLITICAL POWER OF THE ULTRA-Orthodox in a nation founded and maintained almost overwhelmingly by secular pioneers? And how different, really, are the haredim? About two-thirds are descendants of immigrants who followed their rabbis from Eastern Europe to Palestine in the nineteenth century even before the earliest Zionists; most of the others originated in the Middle East. Their Meah She'arim quarter just outside the walls of the Old City was a community planned for only several hundred families. Today, with their strictly religious education, they refuse to blend with other Jews and have turned the rule of the ballot box on its head to preserve extreme minority rights by exploiting the divisions between the secular and religious wings of the Zionist majority, which has never been able to create a durable governing consensus.

When Israelis elected their first parliament after the state was established in 1948, Jews of various political persuasions formed parties that were cross-hatched by economic ideology and religious persuasion—none ever large enough to win an absolute majority. While Zionism was an overarching political movement dedicated to the creation of a Jewish homeland, its committed followers were to be found across a broad spectrum of religious belief. Those who stressed religion as the defining quality of Jewish identity were a distinct minority—and these religious Zionists did not even include the ultra-Orthodox, who rejected the very idea of a Jewish state without a Messiah to govern it. Israel's first prime minister, David Ben-Gurion, the socialist chief of the trade unions and the Labor Party's political machine even before independence, was nobody's idea of a religious Jew. He was rarely seen in synagogue and argued that "a Jew is one who sees himself as a Jew." In this he spoke for the majority of the Zionist settlers, for whom their Jewish identity was defined by ancestry, history, culture, and—not to be forgotten after the Holocaust—the non-Jewish world. On the religious end of the spectrum stood a number of small parties who sought a greater stress on religion in the new state, but even they were subject to splits: the small Zionist Mizrachi Party offshoot was known as the Workers Mizrachi, based largely in towns. The energy of the Zionist movement flowed mainly from the kibbutzim—the collective settlements where Ben-Gurion worked when he arrived from Poland in 1905. Even the nationalists of the right were also overwhelmingly secular. Known as Revisionists, they split with Ben-Gurion over whether to accept a state in Palestine that would be partitioned between Jews and Arabs. Their banner foresaw a Jewish state covering all of Palestine up to and even beyond the Jordan River. Their leader, Ze'ev Jabotinsky, a Russian journalist who never lived to see an independent Israel, argued that Jews who followed the medieval customs of the ultra-Orthodox should not even have the right to vote.

Voters in the new nation fell broadly into varieties of Socialism, liberal capitalism, and nationalism. While several smaller religious parties allied themselves to parties of the left or right, during the first twenty years of Israel's history, left-wing politicians governed with the support of the National Religious Party, which represented observant Jews of Orthodox persuasion and their rabbis—but not the ultras. With the conquest of the West Bank in 1967, the Israeli right wing grew in power by promising to keep the territory captured from Jordan and loosen controls over Israel's economy. The right attracted an increasingly urban population, and the religious parties accordingly turned right as well. The National Religious Party withered away as Israeli politics became more divisive, and the ultra-Orthodox Agudat Israel (Israel Association) allied itself with the Shas Party, composed mostly of immigrants from Muslim countries. Although some Shas supporters are not ultra-Orthodox, they are among Israel's most vociferous voters and follow the party's platform with religious commitment. Shas has grown by challenging the Eastern European establishment to end job discrimination and vigorously advocating Israel's permanent control of the territories conquered in the Six-Day War of 1967.

In the more than sixty years of its existence, Israel has been continuously ruled by secular governments. In national elections, religious parties have never come close to obtaining a majority of the votes. Yet, since 1977, when Menachem Begin first gained power, this minority has almost always gotten its way. Only rarely has the majority joined forces across the aisle to oppose the religious parties on their particular issues. Even more rarely do they enact laws over religious objection. Late in 2010, seventy-five Knesset members, a two-thirds majority, voted for preliminary adoption of a law that would enable the military rabbinate to approve the formal conversion of soldiers who had passed courses in Judaism without the supervision of the chief rabbinate. The religious parties immediately threatened a government crisis if the law was finally approved. Thus they blocked the road to full citizenship for thousands of young immigrants from the old

Soviet Union who could not prove their Jewish ancestry but were nevertheless fulfilling the most important duty of Israeli citizenship, from which the ultra-Orthodox ironically remain exempt.

Such political brinksmanship by the religious parties is generally waged by trading their votes for concessions in several broad areas—budget policy, social behavior, and marriage and divorce. Above all, the religious minority has always demanded and usually obtained specific subsidies to operate its separate education system and support more than one hundred thousand students in religious seminaries with their large families. The state also pays for an elaborate rabbinical bureaucracy as outright patronage. At the demand of the ultras, a legal framework has grown up governing Sabbath observance, kosher food, and not only the most intimate areas of marriage and divorce but its public aspects such as child support and inheritance. The issues are not theological; the aim is simply to reinforce and extend the power of Orthodox rabbis. They do not even demand any sort of religious obligation from secular politicians or from individual voters in performing religious commandments known as mitzvoth.

Disputes over interpretations of Jewish law also turn far less on ideology than on raw power. The question of "Who is a Jew?" has persisted from the early days of the Zionist movement to the present. In 1950 Ben-Gurion's government adopted the Law of Return, which allowed any Jew to settle in the new nation and defined a Jew broadly as anyone with one Jewish grandparent. It was drafted as the mirror image of the Nazi Nuremberg laws, which defined a Jew likewise, and thus the new state cast itself as a safe haven and homeland for anyone who would have been ostracized and possibly murdered in Nazi Germany. Even a judge of the Supreme Court, Dr. Moshe Zilberg, believed that if an immigrant considered himself a Jew and "the immigration authorities were convinced by all reasonable evidence that he is a Jew, the gates of the land would not be closed to him." Only after several lawsuits did the question arise: what is the status of a person who declared himself a Jew but also professed another religion? The specific case involved a Catholic monk, Brother Daniel, who had been born a Jew in Poland, hid in a monastery during the Holocaust, and claimed still to be a Jew despite his conversion. The Supreme Court denied his plea to be recognized officially as a Jew on his identity card but allowed him to remain in Israel. A further question goes to the heart of Israeli identity: what is the link between nationality and religion? Even more complicated is the argument over acceptance of conversion: can one rabbi disqualify another and override his decisions?

From such seemingly arcane questions flow the problem of conversion and the most fundamental right, that of citizenship in a nation founded to shelter and protect Jews. The arguments rarely turn on the morality of any particular decision, but on who has the authority to make them. While some issues are more important than others, the inability to resolve such internal disputes may set off an explosion potentially more dangerous than the continuing external threats to Israel's security. There is no way to measure the long-term damage to Israeli society if the monopoly of the rabbinical courts over family disputes is not broken. And if one-fifth or more of all pupils in Israeli schools do not learn mathematics, English, and civics, part of an entire generation will be dependent on government handouts for the rest of their lives.

UNTIL RECENTLY, ISRAEL'S LEADERS ASPIRED TO CREATE A SECULAR democracy on the Western model and lived like most politicians in Western Europe and America. Many objected to strict Sabbath observance, the rabbinical monopoly over marriage and divorce, and military exemption for yeshiva students. But they were out-maneuvered by the Orthodox bloc in parliament that had learned how to exploit the rivalries among the secular parties. The religious Zionists buried their own differences and in the early days of the state served as interlocutors with the ultra-Orthodox, who did not recognize the state at all. But after the conquests of the Six-Day War expanded Israel's control over all the lands of the Bible in 1967, the religious parties lost their special role in the Zionist movement and turned aggressively expansionist.

Religious Zionists adopted a messianic stance and played a leading role in settling the occupied territories. Far from refusing military service, many of the settlers' sons headed for the elite fighting units that used to be the preserve of the secular sons of the kibbutz. In its commitment to a Greater Israel that would incorporate large areas of the occupied territories and push out the Palestinians, religious Zionism joined Israel's secular right on its most extreme political flank. At the same time it allied itself with the ultra-Orthodox on some domestic questions. This helped bring the ultra-Orthodox into the political arena; their refusal to recognize the legitimacy of government and its institutions faded. Far from strengthening the state, it split the political establishment on religious lines. Instead of turning their backs on the secular political structure they had disdained, the majority of the ultras began cooperating with the government to obtain financial support. Only a few extreme groups such as the Satmar Hasidim and the Neturei Karta stand outside the state, even to the point of siding with its enemies such as the Islamic regime in Iran. (These groups also stand outside the purview of this book in its examination of the ultra-Orthodox.)

These ties between the religious Zionists and the haredim have gained enough strength to dictate the conduct of many aspects of daily life and to indirectly influence important political decisions. In the private realm, their tactic is to impose restrictions on matters such as Sabbath observance and dietary rules. In the political realm, their tactic is to prevent action on important issues, especially in objecting to territorial concessions to the Palestinians.

Since the dispute between the religious parties and the majority of voters in Israel is not primarily about Jewish law but about political muscle, the prospects are dim for secular Israelis to regain their dominant public voice in making policy. Consider the rise of the Shinui (Change) Party, whose principal goal was to block the increasing influence of the ultrareligious. At its peak in 2003, Shinui had fifteen members in the Knesset, before falling victim to internal disputes that left it unable to deliver on its principal promise to reform the electoral system. Once the Shinui or any other secular politicians joined coalition governments, reforms were blocked by religious parties whose slightest concession would have meant their own political suicide. Left uncertain at this writing is whether the blatant concessions Netanyahu offered to the haredim in blunting the secular demands for their military service will affect the electoral support for his Likud Party in elections that must be held in 2013. Rather than governing from a firmer political base, Netanyahu remained on a tightrope after Kadima abandoned him. His secular nationalist supporters continue to be led by Foreign Minister Avigdor Lieberman, who had threatened to quit the government if too many concessions were granted to the ultras on their virtually nonnegotiable demand for the military exemption. It is profoundly resented by the Russian immigrants, who do their service and whom Lieberman's party represents.

On other issues the religious parties have shown far more flexibility. Even ministers who loudly opposed the application of religious law in civil society were deemed acceptable as political partners of the religious parties in governing coalitions—as long as these ministers agreed to prevent buses from running on the Sabbath and to discriminate against women in matters of marriage and divorce. In the great tradition of Talmudic scholars, they were willing to split hairs on the letter of religious observance while letting its spirit die, even in places such as the holiest in Judaism, the Western Wall. There the sexes are separated at prayer, and the subsidiary section for women has become a continuing source of controversy. The late Professor Yeshayahu Leibowitz ridiculed the rules imposed on this sacred place by characterizing it as "the discotheque of the Shechinah" (God's spirit). Leibowitz, himself a strictly observant Jew, was also a bitter cynic. He accused Ben-Gurion of refusing to support a formal separation of the state from religion purely in order to prolong the fight between secular and religious Jews.

But in fact religious politicians refused to rise to the bait of this supposed distraction and avoided confrontation. Their strategy of compromise and coalition enabled them to advance to positions of influence, which led to gradual but decisive political victories. Israel still does not have a constitution defining the rights of the individual. Religious education thrives with state subsidy. Ultra-Orthodox Jews escape military service. Women suffer discrimination in marriage and especially divorce because they are governed by religious law defining males as dominant and even decisive in many areas of life. Orthodox tradition and practice have increasingly influenced the pace of daily life in Jerusalem, Israel's capital, while Tel Aviv and Haifa are bustling Mediterranean cities as modern as Barcelona. And these barriers against modernity remain firmly in place despite the religious parties' stagnating parliamentary representation.

For decades Israeli voters have never given more than four or five seats to parties allied to Agudat Israel, the oldest party representing only the ultra-Orthodox and their flag-carriers in the political wars. The Shas Party, led by ultra-Orthodox rabbis and militantly anti-Arab as the spokesmen for the Sephardic Jews forced out of their homes elsewhere in the Middle East, reached its high-water mark of fifteen parliamentary seats in 2003, but it has been receding since despite the steady demographic increase of the ultras. And the National Religious Party, originally Labor's ally, has almost completely disappeared. Why have their supporters not rewarded them with more seats?

The explanation lies in the voting habits of the young. After military service, many appear to have withdrawn support for the religious parties and shifted to the nationalist right. In theory, the religious parties should be able to maintain their electoral strength simply because their high birth rate produces enough voters to offset the low turnout among haredi women. But in fact they are losing voters to the largely secular nationalist parties of the right, principally the Likud of Netanyahu and the late Menachem Begin. To hold the loyalty of their new supporters among the ultra-Orthodox, Likud doles out subsidies. It maintains welfare payments to the large haredi families and helps their schools escape state supervision. In return, the ultra-Orthodox support these right-wing nationalists even though their Revisionist founder Jabotinsky regarded the haredim as obscurantist and wanted nothing to do with them. Having cut their ties with the left, all the religious parties have become part of a rightward realignment in Israel that decreases the likelihood of the left regaining power. Labor can no longer depend on Israeli Arab voters. They now constitute almost 20 percent of the electorate and vote for parties that support Arab nationalist causes, to which most

Israelis object. Such divisiveness leaves the Arabs out of the main-stream political dialogue in a country where they are a distinct minority that must defend itself against Jewish nationalists.

Shas therefore has had to fight to keep its Middle Eastern immigrant base from drifting toward Likud. It has done so by adopting the more extreme anti-Arab positions of the secular right-wing parties on expanding Jewish settlements in the West Bank and building houses for Jews in the Arab sections of Jerusalem. This political tilt holds dire implications for the American-sponsored process designed to bring peace between Israel and the Palestinians. Trading land to bring the principal settlements formally inside Israeli territory as part of delineating the borders of two distinct states would be anathema to the nationalist Israeli right, because the remaining Jewish settlers would be forced either to withdraw from their isolated West Bank outposts or become part of a Palestinian state.

In the parliamentary elections of 2009, the drift of the haredim toward the right gathered momentum. As a direct result, the Shas political leader Eli Yishai, a deputy prime minister, became one of the most outspoken opponents of the West Bank construction freeze demanded by the Obama administration, even though this opposition meant endangering Israel's relations with the United States. Nevertheless, the haredim have hedged their bets. Two weeks after the founder of Shas, the charismatic Rabbi Ovadia Yosef, publicly raged against the Palestinians and their leaders, he sent a conciliatory message to Hosni Mubarak, then Egypt's president, expressing his hopes for peace between Israel and all the Arabs.

But the chokehold of the religious parties in the Knesset remains although the names and leaders have changed over the years. Their total representation in the Knesset has swung from ten members in the early 1980s to a peak of twenty-nine in 1999, and then down to eleven a decade later. Yet their power has grown steadily, in part through their alliances with the religious Zionists; their refusal to compromise on their basic demands is combined with their tactic of achieving success by trading votes on other issues. Even the addition of several hundred thousand immigrant voters from the former Soviet Union has not undermined the strength of the religious bloc, although perhaps as many as one-third of the immigrants claiming Jewish ancestry upon arrival in Israel were actually born Christian, and most of the remainder barely observe Jewish law and ritual.

A new and still untested factor is the social upheaval of 2012, in which hundreds of thousands protested the inequality of Israeli society that has resulted from Benjamin Netanyahu's market-oriented economic policies, first as finance minister and then as prime minister. He at first tried to mollify the middle classes with a housing bill targeting young working families with government loans that, unlike grants to the haredim accounting for a large part of the housing budget, offered some likelihood of being repaid. The haredi parties blocked the bill. This time Netanyahu refused to give in. The whole bill, which included essential amendments to the government's housing policy, had to be dropped, but the battle had been joined. A spokesman for the prime minister told a television reporter: "Don't worry, the rabbis will have to learn to do with less."

But the rabbis had tested their strength and won; they used their political muscle again to hold on to the military exemption that is deplored by the great majority of Israelis. Until that moment, Netanyahu was seen standing at the peak of his political career by most supporters and opponents alike. The strongest countries in the Arab world, Egypt and Syria, were torn apart by deep internal disputes, with Syria heading toward civil war; the Palestinians were deadlocked and the peace process stalled, and Israel's most threatening enemy, Iran, was squeezed by sanctions that punished the nation for their leaders' drive toward nuclear weapons. At home, Netanyahu's policies had laid the foundation for growth based on sound financial management and techno- logical miracles of innovation admired the world over. He then capped these successes by assembling the largest parliamentary coalition that had ever supported any Israeli prime minister. No wonder that both U.S. presidential candidates seemed desperate for his support, and the international press expected great things. *Time* magazine's cover story, written by its managing editor, anointed him "Bibi, King of the Jews."

Few crowned heads have been dethroned more quickly. Recognizing that the economy might be heading for trouble, Netanyahu knew he had to propose budget cuts and unpopular tax increases that would need the votes of his grand coalition in the Knesset. Although Kadima's price for joining the coalition had been an end to the haredi military exemption, this overconfident political tactician gambled that he could hold together his over- whelming parliamentary majority even if he yielded to the rab- bis on this incendiary issue. In losing this gamble, Netanyahu foreclosed opportunities to address grave challenges at home and abroad and demonstrated a lack of conviction and a loss of nerve that are inexcusable failures in a national leader.

Clearly the growing divisions within such a small and homogeneous country are unsustainable. Stanley Fischer, the gov- ernor of the Bank of Israel, which plays a broader role in manag- ing the economy than most central banks in other countries, summoned ultra-Orthodox leaders in the autumn of 2010 and warned them that the nation cannot afford to continue subsidizing their unproductive way of life. Members of the Jerusalem City Council, as well as parents of soldiers, economists, and journalists have sounded a similar alarm. But the government has been grid-locked by the political power of the ultra-Orthodox. The one positive sign is the small but growing number of young haredim trying to break the mold by pursuing academic and vocational studies leading to employment.

Many believe that the haredim's confidence in their ability to maintain their special status and subsidies is grounded in the fear of losing control over their younger generation. Yet, while all secular parties agree that there is an urgent need to limit the concessions won by the ultra-Orthodox over many years, few agree on how to do it. Netanyahu and his Likud Party claim to support gradual change in the hope that delay will mollify their ultra-Orthodox allies while not alienating the party's secular base. But the facts prove otherwise: the coalition with the Kadima Party broke up after only seventy days when Netanyahu attempted to impose gradualism and his secular partners rejected it. This very breakup seemed to have cemented the bond between Israel's political right and its religious extremists into a lasting political reality. The test between these allied political and religious extremists on one side and the more moderate secularists on the other is likely to be played out at the ballot box. Just as the Zionists believe they are forging the future for the Jews, the ultras are equally certain that they own the future because they are grounded in the long history of the Jews.

Except for Netanyahu's followers, the other secular parties argue that gradualism is pointless and that urgent reforms are necessary to remove economic and social constraints in a modern nation. They want to strengthen civil society against a vociferous minority that refuses to recognize the legitimacy of a democrat-

37

ically elected government and rejects any duty to defend it against enemies who would destroy them and all other Israeli Jews—as well as the state that protects and even nurtures the parallel society they have created in the name of a higher power to which they pledge total allegiance. At the same time, they reach out from their cloistered society and attempt to impose fundamentalist values and practices on a secular majority that has rejected them since the rise of modern Zionism a century ago. With the founding of Israel, many of these contradictions were finessed and the argument over them largely subdued. But as the tyranny of this religious minority asserts itself more aggressively, the debate over its role in public and private life in Israel will play a determining role in the future of the state and its security in the Middle East.

2

How the War Began

THE BITTER CONFLICT BETWEEN ISRAEL'S SECULAR MAJORITY and its ultra-Orthodox minority has gathered force in the years of our new century and especially during the years of Netanyahu's government. Its origins can be traced back more than three centuries to the rise of the Enlightenment. Although Jews were then living mostly in closed communities across Europe, they nevertheless were swept along as this turn away from medieval religious authority toward human reason infiltrated European society and brought with it, in its second wave, the origins of nationalism. The Jews even adopted their own Hebrew word for the Enlightenment—*haskalah*. But even though the movement was rooted in rational thought and political ideology, the conflicts within the Jewish world that now seem to be reaching their peak have always been less ideological than practical: who shall have control over the Jewish masses?

Until their political emancipation at the start of the nineteenth century across most of Western Europe, most Jews lived secluded from Christian society in the ghettos in the Middle Ages, in the small towns of Eastern Europe known as shtetls, and in their own neighborhoods of Western Europe, where the boundaries were gated by psychology and custom rather than wood and iron. Inside these enclaves they maintained their Talmudic studies and their special professions. This professional and physical separation helped them to avoid assimilation; even the dietary laws played a role because observant Jews could not join in the many social rituals celebrated with food and drink. But the Enlightenment opened the possibility of breaking these barriers. Moses Mendelssohn (1729–1786), the German philosopher and merchant whose wisdom was revered by his Christian contemporaries, was among the first to attempt to forge a link between reason and religious belief.

Soon nationalism and the ensuing emancipation started the integration of the Jewish masses into European and American societies. Yet, for the two groups among the Jews, the Zionists and the rigorously observant Orthodox, the solution was not assimilation but redemption. Zionists believed that they would be redeemed by returning to their ancestral home, Zion, the Land of Israel, and rebuilding it by their own hard work. For the Orthodox, redemption meant the miraculous arrival of the Messiah, who would gather all Jews back to the land of their forefathers. As most scholars see it, Zionism supplied the essential elements lacking in the rational and individualistic ideas of the Enlightenment by creating a new unity between being a "Jew" and "human being." Under their prophet, Theodor Herzl (1860–1904), the Zionists became a political movement that was soon composed of two main branches: secular and religious Zionists. Neither believed that redemption would come by miracles but by building and defending the Jewish homeland. But the religious wing of the movement stressed the observance of Jewish law and custom while toiling like their more secular brothers and sisters to make the desert bloom.

Ironically, the ancient homeland of Eretz Israel became a battleground between both wings of the Zionist movement and what we now call the ultra-Orthodox, some of whom had actually preceded Herzl's followers to the Promised Land. These early arrivals came in small groups during the middle of the nineteenth century, ostensibly to protect themselves from assimilation in Europe. Both Zionist wings later found themselves fighting the ultra-Orthodox over their way of life; the battlefields extended to education, women's rights, government budgets, and military service.

Zionism drew together many historic, religious, and philosophical strands. Hundreds and then thousands of mainly young people established agricultural settlements. They were encouraged to build the new Jewish nation by physical labor and to revive the ancient Hebrew language in what was then a backwater of the Ottoman Empire. But by far the greater part of the Jewish Diaspora rejected the Zionist call to return to the land that God had promised the Jews through this largely secular optic; on the contrary, huge waves fled Europe to escape persecution and seek opportunity in the New World. A minority believed that they could remain in the Diaspora and build a society based on ancient Jewish law—halacha—until the arrival of the Messiah would bring them miraculously to the Holy Land. Others believed they could help rebuild European society on more just foundations through socialism.

Zionist thinkers realized that their ideology was based on a contradiction. As part of the Enlightenment movement, they had abandoned an absolute belief in divine authority and made man the source of the guidance that directed them to leave the Diaspora and build a new life in the Land of Israel. Their religious opponents argued that Jewish tradition forbade *dehikat ha-ketz*,

41

which loosely translated means interfering with the Divine Will that determines the arrival of the Messiah. History was supposed to end only when the Messiah came, and meanwhile life would be focused on waiting and praying for this transcendent event.

As a political movement, Zionism set out to resist the threat to Jewish culture as it had been known until the middle of the nineteenth century but also the threat to the physical existence of Jews in Europe. Herzl, who founded Zionism at the turn of the twentieth century long before the Holocaust, despaired of the European establishment accepting Jews with full rights. He wrote: "If I knew assimilation would succeed, I would have asked the Pope to convert all the Jews to Christianity." A successful Viennese journalist born in Budapest, Herzl thus encountered the Zionist idea by way of a pragmatic, almost cynical, approach. It was cemented by the Dreyfus case in France, which Herzl reported for his newspaper once it became a cause célèbre for French intellectuals who were fighting to shake off the influence of the church and its prejudices in the life of the French Republic. If an army officer named Alfred Dreyfus from an old French-Jewish family could be persecuted, stripped of his rank, sent to Devil's Island as a spy, and not even pardoned after evidence proved him innocent of espionage, then, Herzl concluded, there was no room for Jews to assimilate in European society, and they had to settle in their own ancestral land.

Socialism offered another solution, which at the end of the nineteenth century led to the formation in Eastern Europe of the Bund—the German word for league. But these radical young Jews soon saw the true nature of the new Bolshevik regime and tried to merge their Socialist ideals with Jewish cultural traditions and the Yiddish language. The Bund then became a league of committed Jewish Socialists. Up until the outbreak of World

War II, many more Jews supported the Bund than supported the Zionist parties in Poland, the country with the largest and most active Jewish population. Mass emigration also brought the movement to the United States, where it was called the Arbeiter Ring—the Workers' Circle—boasting schools, summer camps, and a strong belief in secular Judaism and social justice in their adopted country.

The spirit of change also penetrated the ultra-Orthodox movements. In direct contradiction to the ideology of Agudat Israel that the return to Zion must await the coming of the Messiah, other ultra-Orthodox Jews began arriving there from Europe. During the 1840s and 1850s, immigrants enlarged Jerusalem's tiny Jewish community, which lived for the most part inside the walls of the Old City. While this immigration was a natural development of the rising sense of nationalism in Europe, for the ultra-Orthodox it required some kind of apology. The traditional excuse was that the arrivals came to pray and die in the Holy Land, not to build a new life there. With that as their rationale, they felt they had every right to expect full support from Diaspora Jews, who would benefit indirectly from their prayers in the holy city of Jerusalem and thus speed the arrival of the Messiah.

One authority on modern Jewish history, Israel Bartal of Jerusalem's Hebrew University, argues that not only was there a "pull" drawing ultra-Orthodox Jews to pray in the holy city, but also a "push" driving them there—their fear that emancipation was fostering assimilation that was undermining even the most traditional communities of Eastern Europe. Hence they fled to Zion to guard their identity. The largest group to arrive in the 1840s came from Lithuania, mainly scholarly disciples of HaGaon Rabbi Eliyahu, the spiritual leader of the Vilna yeshiva, who was known as the Gara—an honorific meaning "genius." The rabbi's followers were renowned for their opposition to the Hasidim, who approached God by singing and dancing as well as praying. Hence they were known as the Mitnagdim—the Oppositionists—for their devotion to intellectual study and life. The descendants of these orthodox immigrants from Lithuania, known today as the Litaim, are the extremists among the haredim. Other groups, less devoted to study of the Talmud but more dependent on their spiritual leaders, soon arrived mainly from Poland and Galicia to form Jerusalem's ultra-Orthodox community.

Contributions to help support these pious arrivals came from abroad, the ultras in effect levying a tax on European congregations to support the meager lives of the Jerusalem Jews. Each month a portion was handed out in a *halukah*—distribution— on the basis of how much had been contributed in each family's native land. But the sums were relatively small and could not save them from poverty. Many were forced to work, often at the expense of their studies and prayers. Although some established businesses in trade or personal services, a growing percentage remained dependent on help from outside the community. And today the haredim are almost totally dependent on the budget of the State of Israel for their subsistence and on contributions from abroad to support their yeshivot.

Once established, members of the ultra-Orthodox community aspired to an exemplary life of prayer and study in the Holy Land. But in fact, throughout the newly expanded Jewish world in Palestine, the many competing sects were renowned for infighting that prevented their members from uniting under one leadership, even when faced with an existential crisis by the collapse of the Ottoman Empire during World War I. Within that multiethnic empire, they had a legally defined place as a recognized community. And as a society of scholars they received economic support from the Diaspora, although it never succeeded in offering meaningful guidance to world Jewry. This absence of competition prevented progress in the community, and the better elements drifted away. This steady desertion in turn strengthened the non-Orthodox community, which offered greater possibilities to more ambitious refugees from ultra-Orthodox control.

Nevertheless, the haredi community in Jerusalem proved more durable than commonly believed because it survived the control of Palestine between the wars under the British mandate, despite its loss of official recognition. When things changed radically in 1948, and Israel shook off foreign rule, the haredim were able not only to link themselves to the new state by taking its subsidies but also to expand as their needs grew. Some social scientists argue that a community like this, in need of constant support to grow, is not necessarily weak because it draws its strength from its internal cohesion.

The small haredi community, separated by its own choice from Jewish and Zionist politics and more inclined to be seen as a special community by the British mandate authorities, did not receive much attention at first from the leaders of the secular Zionist parties. Only after the establishment of the state in 1948, its founder, David Ben-Gurion, clearly formulated the paradox of political Zionism. He often said: "Two basic aspirations are the background for our work in this land—one, to be like all other nations, and the other, to be different from all other nations." He included the haredi minority in this paradox. Zionism has always been shot through with contradictions. Political leaders like Ben-Gurion adopt the spirit and rhetoric of nineteenth-century Europe's revolutionary movements while perhaps even unconsciously seeking to build institutions in the spirit of the community they knew in the past.

Nothing could embody this contradiction more successfully than the kibbutz, which was the early model for Israeli society and produced many of its leaders, while the haredim looked and behaved like leftovers from Diaspora Judaism.

Under Ben-Gurion's leadership, the majority of the settlers were secular and made Hebrew a living language to unify their community and help establish its identity for nationhood, meanwhile maintaining Jewish traditions including the celebration of the weekly Sabbath and other holy days. They believed that revival in the lands of the Bible would prevent the loss of Jewish identity and the absorption into a non-Jewish majority that threatened Diaspora Jews, even the religious ones. A second group stressed more rigorous preservation of tradition but believed in a practical Zionism by settling in the Land of Israel. The third group, the haredim, was represented by the Agudat Israel Party and rejected Zionism; these believers urged all Jews to concentrate on praying for the arrival of the Messiah.

These three groups exist to this day, more than a century after the emergence of the Zionist idea. The argument among them has not been settled and now threatens the unity of Israeli society more than ever as all three evolve into distinct camps. The secularists believe that they have succeeded in maintaining Jewish linguistic and intellectual heritage while simultaneously integrating its accomplishments into the Western mainstream. This goal has surely been achieved by the worldwide recognition of Israeli authors and scientists, to say nothing of the military accomplishments of the state. But at the same time, the gap between the religious Zionists and the haredim has narrowed considerably with the establishment of settlements in the occupied territories after the Six-Day War: the inheritors of Jabotinsky's nationalism joined with an aggressive settler movement that

David Ben-Gurion, founder of the State of Israel

appealed to the religious strain in Zionism for its emphasis on re-claiming the lands of the Bible—all of them. The third group, the ultra-Orthodox haredim, has strictly followed the traditional way of life led by their ancestors in the small communities of Eastern Europe before the intellectuals and Zionists fled or were mur-dered en masse during World War II. But to the degree that the ultras participate in Israeli politics, they ally themselves with the nationalist right.

Before Herzl's secular Zionism took hold early in the twen-tieth century, the Zionist influence on Jewish masses was mainly spiritual. The Jewish communities of Europe recognized that the Zionist cause was weak and that their general movement of *hibat Zion*—love of Zion—would gain more from unity. Orthodox rabbis appealed for an end to quarrels with the haredim and even vehemently opposed secular Jewish leaders such as Moshe Leib Lilienblum, who operated in Russia's Pale of Settlement and objected to any ideological struggle against religion lest it impede the return to Zion. For example, he was not opposed to separate secular and religious educational institutions as long as they did not divide into two camps that would bar marriage among adherents of each group. Even within the Orthodox there was a movement toward cooperation led by Rabbi Abraham Isaac HaCohen Kook, the chief rabbi under the British mandate, who tried to build bridges among the secular and religious Zionists and even the ultras by preaching that all who helped reestablish Jewish rule in the Holy Land were promoting the arrival of the Messiah.

Nineteenth-century Zionism was always a minority movement because other choices were open to the Jewish masses who rebelled against the physical and spiritual poverty of life in Eastern Europe. They could immigrate to America and other distant continents. They could also join revolutionary movements in Europe or assimilate in bourgeois society. Moving either to the secular left or right, they hoped to escape anti-Semitism by joining in the culture and economic activity of the non-Jewish majority. The relatively small part of European Jewry that stubbornly kept to the strict framework of traditional Jewish observance needed to separate itself from secular society in order to guard its distinctiveness, not only to follow religious commandments but also to preserve its way of life. That meant different clothing, separate schools, and even separate neighborhoods wherever possible.

*Rabbi Abraham Isaac HaCohen Kook, chief Rabbi and unrivaled leader of the ortho-
doxy until his death in 1934. Although he, like most of his haredi followers, yearned
for the arrival of the Messiah, he respected the Zionists who came to till the soil. His
son, Rabbi Tzvi Yehuda Kook, became the spiritual guide of the young settlers of the
West Bank after the Six-Day War in 1967.*

This minority constructed its own ideological framework
by founding Agudat Israel in 1912, even before Britain's Balfour
Declaration offered a homeland for Jews four years later. Holding
fast to their belief that only the Messiah could bring true redemption, the party commanded its followers to cling to their
traditions, wait, and pray. Many truly believed that their prayers literally beckoned the Messiah, and that those who did not follow
their path delayed his return. Most Jews decided mainly to wait,

but not necessarily to pray. In the big cities of Europe and America, secular Jewish life strengthened and became more attractive. In Warsaw, just before World War II, the Jewish population had grown to more than three hundred thousand, but the haredim remained an increasingly small minority. In New York, the prewar world's other great Jewish city, haredim were rare, old, and dying off until the Holocaust prompted a postwar revival among the young seeking a sense of community solidarity and protection in a competitive and secular culture.

But the nationalist movement developed more slowly in Eastern Europe, where the influence of the liberal inheritors of the Enlightenment demanding a break with the past and freedom for ethnic communities was weaker than in Western Europe. The difference in the speed of change can be seen in the rise of Zionism. In Eastern Europe a kind of practical Zionism developed, and most of those who first reached Palestine from the East in the 1880s were farmers. They brought with them their traditional religious framework and constituted what is known as the First Aliyah—the Hebrew word for "ascension." They observed the religious commandments and immediately built synagogues that became the centers of community life.

By contrast, in Western Europe Herzl's Zionism looked toward the creation of a new political society in the Land of Israel. In the next wave of immigration during the first decade of the twentieth century—the Second Aliyah—Jews arrived under the influence of the revolutionary trends that had begun to shape modern Europe and thought of themselves as workers; unfortunately many of them soon left for America. Those who stayed were among the founders of the first kibbutzim. After World War I the secular forces of Palestine were augmented by refugees from the Bolshevik revolution in Russia. Finally came sixty thousand immigrants from Germany, Austria, and Czechoslovakia during the 1930s. Except for a small haredi community from Frankfurt, they had broken with religious tradition well before, especially in Germany. There, Reform Judaism had eased the integration of the Jewish community into secular life and mainstream culture until the rise of Nazism.

The work of Hebrew writers and poets of that period reflects their internal struggle between the attractions of a secular life and their religious roots. Haim Nachman Bialik had been a student in the Wolozhin yeshiva in western Russia but also a Zionist and secularist all his adult life. His poetry brings his readers back to his study hall to understand how the victims of the Kishinev pogrom in 1905 found the strength of spirit to keep up hope despite the murder and pillage all around them. "Heaven, take pity and find a path for me." Shaul Tchernikovsky, a medical student in Heidelberg at the same time, reached the opposite conclusion in a poem that made a strong impression on a generation of pioneers in Palestine by invoking the beauty and strength of Apollo. He contrasted the Greek god with the God of the Jews who had "imprisoned him in the straps of tefillin"—the Jewish regalia worn for daily prayers.

Although they were in the minority, followers of the leftist youth movement Hashomer Hatzair—the Youth Guard—dedicated themselves to getting "free of the burden of religion." Founded in Poland after World War I, the movement spread across Europe and to Palestine. One of the founders, Meir Ya'ari, said he was married by a rabbi mainly to avoid offending his father. But in Palestine the Hashomer Hatzair's Kibbutz Artzi was a partner in the effort of the entire kibbutz movement to create new forms to preserve Jewish tradition. They composed special texts for celebrating Passover in the spring and the autumn harvest festivals. But outside the kibbutz, the secular majority was even less ritualistic and largely apathetic toward formal religion. Observant Jews stood by tradition, which meant Orthodox practice. Without the Conservative and Reform synagogues that were simultaneously attracting most American Jews, the Jews of Palestine were predominantly nonobservant, giving rise to a cynical Israeli saying whose rejection of organized Judaism in the succinct paradox typical of Talmudic prose cannot be fully captured in English: "The synagogue to which I do not go is Orthodox."

A British sociologist, Grace Davie, coined the phrase "belonging without believing" to describe the behavior of most English communicants, who connect to their local church mainly to mark the occasions of a family birth, marriage, and death— or, in the phrase of disappointed English vicars, when they are "hatched, matched, and dispatched." Emanuel Gutmann, an Israeli expert in the sociology of religion, modifies the formula to "belonging without behaving" to explain why secular Jews the world over accept such clearly religious observances as circumcision but do not observe the complex ritual commandments demanding daily observance.

When the State of Israel was established, the secular inhabitants and the religious Zionists were a clear majority of the six hundred Jews, not only in number but in their influence on the life of the new nation. Most of the party leaders were secular and some of them even vehemently antireligious, most notably Ben-Gurion himself. He and his wife Pola had been married in a civil ceremony in New York, where they were living. Ben-Gurion wrote in his diary that registering at city hall made him a quarter of an hour late for a Zionist meeting. Even after returning to Palestine, Ben-Gurion refused to have a religious ceremony. He scorned conversion rites prescribed by the rabbis, arguing that formal conversion is not even mentioned in the Bible's Book of Ruth, which tells the story of the Moabite woman who follows her Jewish mother-in-law Naomi after the death of her husband.

For Ben-Gurion, to be a Jew it was not only sufficient but preferable to live in the Land of Israel and speak Hebrew rather than live in the Diaspora. Ritual meant virtually nothing to him. He opposed the regulations governing kosher food and inveighed against "holy objects," refusing to wear a knitted skullcap known as a *kippah*—a symbol of religious nationalism—or tack to his front door a traditional *mezuzah*—a small container bearing a sacred word or a prayer. At home he ate bread instead of matzoh during Passover and scorned the ritual of making kitchen utensils kosher before the holiday. He did not observe the Sabbath nor preside at the traditional family meal on the eve of the Sabbath nor observe the rest day's many restrictions. With all his respect for the wisdom of the Bible, he did not regard it as a holy text and refused to swear with his hand on it. When the first disputes inevitably erupted over the introduction of "Jewish tradition" in the school system after the creation of the new state, he would not use that term and demanded emphasis on "the great spiritual heritage of the Jewish people."

None of that prevented him as prime minister from forming a governing coalition with the religious Zionist parties, and he was among those who drew up the "status quo" arrangement with the religious factions establishing the Jewish character of the state upon which their special privileges depend to this day. Always a pragmatist when it came to establishing and strengthening the new state, Ben-Gurion saw no contradiction between his personal opposition to ritual observance and the need to ensure the widest political support for the state itself.

Golda Meir—once praised by Ben-Gurion for her resolute

character as "the only man in my cabinet"—also opposed putting the force of law behind Judaism and advocated a separation of religion from the state on the American model. Before her emigration from the United States, she insisted on a civil marriage over her mother's objections. In the early days of the state, she favored a constitution with a formal separation of religious and civil authority, vehemently attacked the religious coercion implicit in personal status laws, and demanded legislation permitting civil as well as religious marriage. "We, the secular public, have not sold our souls," she argued. "The rights of women must be safeguarded under the law."

But once in power, she was forced to compromise, just like her mentor Ben-Gurion. In 1972 the Independent Liberal Party prepared a law relaxing some strictures on religious marriage at the urging of Gideon Hausner, a minister in the Meir government and a former attorney general celebrated for prosecuting Adolf Eichmann. The bill would have enabled "those forbidden to wed" (such as a member of a priestly Kohen family and a divorcée) to marry at the rabbinate in a civil ceremony. Although this would have been a relatively minor exemption, she had to persuade the Liberals to drop their law because it would have endangered her government coalition. She rationalized her opposition to any change in matrimonial law on the basis of national rather than religious considerations—in effect arguing that the state should not intrude on religion and thus turning the idea of civil and religious separation on its head.

Especially outspoken in his opposition to religious legislation in Israel was Pinchas Lavon, secretary of the Histadrut labor union federation and later a cabinet minister. As agriculture minister he ensured the import of nonkosher meat. When the government banned public transport on the Sabbath, he argued, "I can travel on the Sabbath because I have a car. But someone who does not have a car or who cannot afford to pay a taxi cannot travel on the Sabbath. This is a most severe blow against the interests of the multitudes, the rights of the individual and freedom in the State." But the leaders of the party were far from unanimous; some were traditional, and most kept contact with religious leaders.

Even as politics in Israel veered right, nationalist leaders betrayed their own founders when they sought support from religious parties and especially from the ultras. Jabotinsky's Revisionist movement was the forerunner of the Herut Party headed by Menachem Begin. Tzipi Livni, who headed the Kadima Party when it polled the highest number of votes in the 2009 election, is a product of the Revisionist movement through her father, Eitan Livni, operations officer of the underground Irgun and a Herut member of the Knesset. In Jabotinsky's view, religion was the only way for the Jews to preserve their national character in the Diaspora, when they lacked territorial sovereignty. So when the Jewish nation returned from exile, he insisted, religion should return to its earlier role and no longer needed to serve as a framework that divided it from other nations.

Jabotinsky himself was raised in a liberal interpretation of the Torah that separates the external signs and framework of religion from the daily life of the state. Back in their ancient land, he argued, there was no need for Jews to set themselves apart by wearing a fringed undershirt known as a little tallit, or by growing long sidelocks as a sign of piety to the outside world. In a signature essay, "Outside the Encampment," that he published in 1919 in the newspaper *Ha'aretz*, the Revisionist leader warned that "we will announce that those Jews who do not remove the rust of the exile from themselves and refuse to shave their beard and sidelocks will be second-class citizens. They will not be given

the right to vote." He argued that Zionism would end the suffer-
ing of the Diaspora and provide a new direction for spiritual
independence and renewal that had been frozen in centuries of
exile. He insisted on the individual's freedom to practice religion,
demanded it be protected from the Jewish nature of the state, and
he missed no opportunity to speak of a future "Hebrew state"—
not a Jewish state. As a political leader with liberal beliefs, he not
only opposed religious coercion by the rabbis but the antireligious coercion he saw in Communist states.

Even among the General Zionists there were those who
advocated a secular life in the Land of Israel. Yitzhak Gruenbaum,
one of the leaders of Polish Jewry and of the radical wing of the
General Zionists, had been a member of the Polish parliament
from 1919 until 1932, when he left for Palestine. There he continued his fight to separate religion from the state. In 1943 he was
chosen as the head of the Rescue Committee of the Jewish
Agency, the representative of the Jewish community in Palestine
and the governing body of the Zionist movement. He was
arrested by the British in 1946 and imprisoned in Latrun along
with Moshe Sharett and other leaders. Despite his central position
in the leadership of the Jews under the mandate, Gruenbaum was
not among the signers of the Declaration of Independence,
because he refused to be evacuated from besieged Jerusalem in
order to attend the ceremony in Tel Aviv. As the first minister of
the interior, Gruenbaum organized the elections to the first Knesset but was not elected himself and continued to be active as a
left-wing Zionist until his death in 1970 at the age of ninety-one.

The Holocaust in Europe only deepened the debate within
the Jewish community of Palestine over the authority of religion.
It strengthened the argument of the secularists who held that Jews
must find ways to survive by their own means in a world where

God could not prevent the murder of millions. Their opponents argued that no effort should be spared to keep alive the traditions of the past lest the murder of the Jews lead to the breakdown of Judaism. Both sides were convinced that history would prove them right and found no reason to compromise. This passionate ideological debate over the role of religion in civil society gave birth to a practical problem of governance: bridging the gap between the two camps so the political and military challenges of the early days of statehood could be managed by a united front of the Jewish people. This they accomplished, beating back the Arab armies not only with aid from Zionist Jews abroad but with the fledgling state's own deft diplomacy, which coaxed arms from great nations with interests in the region and political imperatives to satisfy at home. A victorious and united Israel emerged as a new and vibrant democracy. But the unity forged in the first flush of independence did not last.

3

The Armored Chariots
of the Messiah

WHEN THE BRITISH GOVERNMENT FORMALLY ENDORSED
a "national home for the Jewish people" in 1917, only the
most ardent Zionists regarded the Declaration of Lord
Balfour, then the foreign secretary of the British government, as a
pledge to support a sovereign Jewish state. Palestine was a backwater
in the crumbling Ottoman Empire. Britain and France, looking
toward victory in World War I, were in the process of carving up the
Ottoman territories of the Middle East. While leaders of the Arab
revolt against the Turks were awarded their own states, the British
took Palestine with a mandate from the League of Nations to
administer its mixed population of Jews, Arabs, and assorted Christian sects. They inherited the Ottoman structure of a multicultural
state with each community enforcing its own domestic code and
adjudicating many civil disputes according to religious law and custom. The Arabs lived under sharia codes, but the Jewish community—known as the Yishuv—was split between secularists following
a civil code and those who followed the Jewish law of the Torah and
the Talmud known as halacha. This division bedeviled the movement
toward independence.

The idea of partitioning Palestine into two independent states did not originate with the Jews but with the British. In 1936 Arab terrorists began attacking Jewish settlements and killing Jews. Irregular Jewish forces responded in kind. What the British rechristened as the Arab Revolt and the Jews euphemistically called "the disturbances" prompted the appointment of a royal commission headed by Lord Peel. A lawyer and cabinet minister descended from a great Conservative British political family, he arrived in Palestine within months of the outbreak of violence. In mid-1937, the Peel Commission recommended splitting the territory into two states, with a central corridor from Jerusalem to the seaports that would remain under British jurisdiction.

Rejected by the Arabs, the Peel proposals did little to quell the violence, perhaps in part because they were fervently embraced by David Ben-Gurion as "an opportunity which we had never dared to dream in our wildest imagination . . . more than a state, government, and sovereignty—this is a national consolidation in a free homeland." As head of the Jewish Agency responsible for immigration, he welcomed a Jewish state as a refuge for hundreds of thousands of European Jews who were being impoverished and expelled from German territories by Hitler's government. But there was no such joy among the ultra-Orthodox. Leaders of Agudat Israel appeared before the Peel Commission as representatives of the ultras to express their uncompromising opposition to any Jewish state, and especially to any solution that would not maintain the writ of Jewish law that had passed down from Ottoman rule. As the ultras saw it, the future Jewish state could be established only after the arrival of the Messiah, who would secure the real salvation of the Jewish people. The Royal Commission ignored their arguments against a Jewish state, largely because under its plan the ultra-Orthodox communities would be almost entirely excluded. They were located mainly in Jerusalem, which under the Peel proposals was to remain under British rule.

Once the recommendations of the commission were set aside, this fierce internecine dispute was largely forgotten—but not by Ben-Gurion. Ten years later, when the great debate over statehood took place at the United Nations, the man who would lead Israel to independence remembered how fiercely the ultra-Orthodox had opposed the Peel plan despite their political weakness in Palestine. The Yishuv and its allies in the Diaspora had to fight for the support of every UN member, and until the very last moment when the vote was called in the General Assembly on November 29, 1947, no one could be certain that the partition of Palestine between Jews and Arabs would be approved by the necessary two-thirds supermajority.

In such a situation it was vital to prevent Agudat Israel from once again expressing its opposition to partition, lest that influence Orthodox opinion abroad. To protect his flank, Ben-Gurion took it upon himself to make a deal with Agudat Israel, even though the party had never shown much political muscle before. He would guarantee that in the new state, religious questions would be resolved exactly as they had been under the mandate. There would be no divergence from the "status quo" in religious matters even under a secular government, and he assured the haredim that certain principles regulating important aspects of daily life would be safeguarded—Sabbath observance, dietary laws, marriage and divorce, and education.

Aside from the cliff-hanging UN vote, Ben-Gurion had other reasons to seek an understanding with Agudat Israel. The religious Zionists also welcomed the same standstill, and relations between them and Ben-Gurion's secular majority had greatly improved during the pre-independence mobilization. There were religious units in the Palmach, which were the shock troops of the Yishuv's underground army, known as the Haganah (the Hebrew word for defense). During the fight against the Arabs that became open warfare at the moment of independence in 1948, these observant Jews fought alongside the units of the secular labor movement. Relations with Agudat Israel also improved as the mandate neared its end. Its members operated within the framework of the Haganah, and the ultra-Orthodox fought in the post-independence battles to hold Jerusalem. Avraham Hoizman, a young soldier from Jerusalem's ultra-Orthodox Meah She'arim district, fell in the battle that opened the road to the encircled city. Many members of the Irgun, the underground fighters who regarded partition as a weak compromise, also came from the haredim. All these religious groups would have every reason to argue that their sacrifice deserved to be recognized in the new nation's conduct of its affairs—and so they did in the months leading up to independence.

On June 16, 1947, the board of the Jewish Agency confirmed the agreement on a religious status quo as a declaration of intent rather than a binding document, which at that time could not have been legally enforced. This in time led to misunderstandings and differing interpretations, but the principal political purpose had been achieved: Agudat Israel supported the partition plan and even agreed to join the future Israeli government. The four main elements were:

- The Sabbath was declared a day of rest in the Jewish state. Although not stated specifically, the intent was to prevent public transportation in cities where it had been prohibited under the mandate. In Haifa, buses operated on the

Sabbath—and still do—in order to help residents to move freely on the steep streets of that hilly city. Christians and Muslims would be allowed to observe their own weekly day of rest on Sundays or Fridays.

- Jewish dietary laws would be observed in all official kitchens including those in all military establishments and government offices. Jews there could be served only kosher food.

- Marital status—Jewish marriage and divorce—was to be governed by the rules and traditions of Orthodox Judaism. Certificates for all marriages performed in the new state would have to be signed by Orthodox rabbis; divorces could be granted only by rabbinical courts; and disputes on such domestic matters including child custody had to be decided by religious tribunals. This was done in order to avoid dividing the public into two camps on such fundamental family issues—but in practice that division between religious and secular is exactly what happened.

- Every educational group was guaranteed the full autonomy it had enjoyed under the mandate. The intent was to ensure there that the state would not interfere in religious instruction, with the proviso that all schools would also teach the Hebrew language, history, science, and other subjects to be prescribed by the government's educational authorities.

The imprecise wording naturally bred disputes; every party read its own meaning into the paragraphs of the agreement, especially concerning education. These were not just Talmudic arguments among scholars. They were raised at the highest levels of government, parliament, and the courts and figured in government crises from the early years of statehood to the present day.

In retrospect, it is clear that the existence of the "status quo" agreement did not always help define the ambit of religious and civil influence but gave rise to damaging conflicts, and not just about where to draw boundaries but about fundamental areas of control. The wording contained no long-term vision of how the nascent government would balance the needs and aspirations of the various groups in the population. It merely attempted to solve current problems and avoided basic issues that were bound to arise, such as the rights of women or the role of education in a modern society.

Professor Aviezer Ravitzky, an authority on Judaism at Hebrew University, has argued that the status quo agreement actually created a damaging illusion that problems had been solved rather than papered over: each side shared a common but erroneous conviction that it owned the future, and the other side would disappear. The haredim believed that the idea of a "secular Jew" was an oxymoron and, like other historical accidents, would fade away in the new state as traditional Jewish observance became the rule rather than the exception. By contrast, the secularists were certain the traditional Orthodox Judaism of elaborate ritual, custom, and law was a Diaspora invention to help Jews set themselves apart. Whether on the political right or left, these secular Jews believed that the return to Zion would normalize the Jewish people and modernize their conduct, and that the excessive Diaspora traditions would at least be marginalized if they did not disappear altogether. The language of the status quo agreement was generally too short and imprecise to cover the subjects that deserved much more detailed treatment to prevent future controversy. This failure must be seen against the background of the circumstances; what Ben-Gurion needed was a piece of paper to prevent undermining the Jewish Agency's argument before the

United Nations Commission. Later it turned out that his party would need the support of the Orthodox to form Israel's first government, and the rabbis demanded that the status quo agreement be honored.

Each side had reasons to justify the agreement. Shlomo Zalman Shragai, a leader of the religious Zionists elected mayor of Jerusalem two years after independence, admitted later that his group was relatively weak when the state was created and therefore could not hope for major concessions from the secular side. So they took what they could get. Ben-Gurion believed and often declared that Israel would not be a "nation of halacha," but a "nation of law"—deploying for law the Hebrew word *chok* from the Bible, where it encompasses a broader scope of tradition and common usage than those commandments deemed as divinely inspired. In a letter to Rabbi Yehuda Leib haCohen Fishman, one of the observant members of the Jewish Agency's executive board, the future prime minister explained: "More than once it has been said that this is not a nation of halacha but one of law, but this does not mean that the law will interfere in halachic matters affecting those who live according to its dictates. We guaranteed freedom of conscience and religion in the Declaration of Independence and in all the basic premises of the various governments (including those in which the religious parties participated), and I do not suppose that you think such freedoms are guaranteed to one side only."

The rabbi replied: "I agree to what we proclaimed at the foundation of the state, that our state is not a theocracy, that there would be freedom of conscience and religion, and I would never dare to demand interference in the life of the individual. However, we proclaimed that the State of Israel is the state of the Jews and the continuation of our historic people, connected to the tradition of our fathers and to the unique nature of Jewish history." If he invoked tradition and history in order to find a place within secular authority, many of his colleagues were far more emphatic. Said Rabbi Meir Bar-Ilan, another leader of the religious Zionists: "With the return to our land, there is an obligation to revive Jewish law and not to go astray after other gods."

And so the argument raged as the institutions of the new state took shape. Clearly, these issues should have been thrashed out beforehand and if not fully clarified in a constitution, at least more clearly defined. Because of haredi obstruction, it became clear soon after independence that Israel would not benefit from definitions of the kind written into the American Constitution, and its leaders looked for other legal devices while people simply lost interest in having such a basic document. No constitution settles all such fundamental debates; its purpose is to provide a political and legal framework for them. Like Israel, America's original colonial settlements were founded as places of religious refuge, except for the large land grants in the south and the port of New Amsterdam established by the tolerant Dutch. To avoid the religious wars that had decimated parts of Europe from which they had fled, the drafters of the U.S. Constitution guaranteed the religious neutrality of the state. The role of religion in government is defined with some clarity: Article VI prohibits religion from being a qualification for public office. But even that was not strong enough for the pious citizens of a nation founded as a refuge for what established European churches regarded as deviant sects. The very first of ten amendments, the Bill of Rights, also ensures that the government cannot set up an official church—"an establishment of religion"—that might enforce a government orthodoxy. Arguments may rage about just what that phrase means and how best to apply it in a modern society, and they are pressed by Christian fundamentalists even today, but the historic dispute over the relationship between church and state nevertheless has a clear constitutional reference point. Israel does not have such a document, in large part because religious extremists have blocked it and have preferred to operate under a vague compromise drawn up in political expediency.

These and other letters and declarations on the relationship between Israeli civil law and the religious duties of individual Jews have served mainly to strengthen each side rather than help determine the spiritual and cultural basis for the nascent state. But it is doubtful that Ben-Gurion and his secular supporters had any other option, and that the leaders of the Jewish Agency could have done anything but strike a deal with the intransigent Agudat Israel. Their followers hardly recognized the legitimacy of a Jewish state without the Messiah to lead it. Even before the elections to the founding assembly in 1949, Ben-Gurion reckoned that his Mapai Party would not receive a clear majority and would have to seek political allies from the left or the right.

A partnership with Mapam, the second largest party, had obvious advantages. In those days its members were social democrats, mainly salaried workers and members of communal kibbutzim or moshavim, the latter a less severe form of cooperative settlement and less well known outside Israel. A government of the left could have proclaimed its more secular interpretation of the status quo agreement without making concessions to a religious opposition. But Ben-Gurion did not want to abandon his traditional allies, the religious Zionists. A reshuffling of political forces might have also divided the victorious Israeli army into units of different ideologies, provided Mapam with its own loyal troops, and endangered the security of the tiny new state with geopolitical implications reaching beyond its borders.

As Israel was founded, the Cold War was beginning, and it was not at all clear that the new nation would identify with the West. The Soviet Union, hoping for a Middle East bridgehead among many old Jewish Socialists and Communists who had escaped Stalinist purges and Nazi extermination, strongly supported the creation of Israel in the UN General Assembly. Czechoslovakia, soon to be absorbed into the Soviet bloc, had supplied arms to Israel that helped defeat the invading Arab armies. By contrast, the United States tried to prevent arms shipments to Israel and recognized the new state only after the UN vote.

Bringing Mapam into the government might have brought the young state into the Soviet bloc, a development that Ben-Gurion rightly feared. This soon became apparent when political alignments coalesced into party politics. In theory, Ben-Gurion could have ignored the religious commitments of the status quo agreement by forming a coalition with the right. But such a national unity government was impossible because left and right were literally at war. Ben-Gurion's Haganah forces irrevocably split with the Irgun on whether to accept partition, with the right-wing nationalists demanding a Jewish state that would extend to the Jordan River and even beyond. The Irgun, meanwhile, refused to merge with the Haganah into a united armed force, insisted on maintaining itself as a separate militia, and tried to bring in its own weapons. When a ship christened the *Altalena* (after Jabotinsky's pen name as a journalist) approached Tel Aviv during the first weeks of statehood carrying a cargo of guns for the Irgun, Haganah shore batteries fired on it and sank it. While that established the principle of a unified Israeli Defense Force, the bloody incident bitterly split secular Zionism between left and right.

Only a coalition with the religious parties remained a political possibility for Ben-Gurion, and the religious bloc included not only the ultra-Orthodox Agudat Israel but the National Religious Party. Their price was set in stone: a veto on religious affairs by putting their own nominees in charge of the ministry and a policy based on the status quo agreement as they interpreted it. These political arrangements made the agreement even more intractable because they ignored the cultural roots of Zionism, and for that the Israeli historian Yigal Elam largely blames the religious Zionists. In his book *Judaism as a Status Quo* (2000), Elam writes: "Whereas the nationalist idea with its secular values was a successful synthesis of two basic notions that came to fruition in the Zionist enterprise in the Land of Israel, the religious Zionists could not suggest a better synthesis. Their feet were stuck in the trap of Orthodoxy, while their hands and head and hearts were vacillating over the nationalist side, with its secular and sovereign aspects."

In the founding assembly of 1949, the religious Zionists were strong enough to defeat an ultra-Orthodox demand to deny women the right to vote, but the ultras still could not abide the idea of a secular state. Instead, they had a messianic vision of a state in which there would be a "renewal of the life of Torah." Their vision of the Zionist enterprise was a quite different Jewish renaissance in which the Jewish religion would spread alongside the writ of Jewish law, and both would dominate all aspects of modern life in the new State of Israel. But as Elam warned, the religious Zionists never proposed a way to realize their dream and never dared to go beyond the formal limits of halacha. They accepted the authority of Orthodox rabbis, who themselves were unable to revolutionize understanding of the Torah and never tried to break the narrow framework of the status quo. Religious Zionists seemed to be hoping for some miraculous redemptive process to sanctify a renewal of the laws and teachings of the Torah.

But if they really intended to block some of its distinctly anti-modern aspects, they would have had to depend on the secular parties to enforce military service on thousands of yeshiva students and restrain the rabbis from enforcing an increasingly complex conversion process.

Whether recognition of the status quo agreement was a pragmatic compromise that permitted all parties to join in founding the state, or simply a colossal political miscalculation by Ben-Gurion and his allies, the fact is that the founders did not achieve a political truce even in the short run. The observant members of the Knesset, especially the religious Zionists, realized that the government was far from committed to the spread of halacha. They adopted a policy of constant pressure and threats for the government to subsidize their way of life and help spread their social agenda. Ben-Gurion soon realized that, even with the absorption of hundreds of thousands of mainly secular Holocaust survivors, the religious bloc would not just fade away. The postwar ingathering of persecuted exiles from devastated Europe was soon followed by hundreds of thousands of Jews who fled or were expelled from Muslim countries in retaliation for Israel's rise as a state. The religious politicians viewed these immigrants from the Middle East and the Mediterranean basin as natural reinforcements even though not all had religious backgrounds.

After generations of applying the agreement and even weaving it into laws covering daily conduct, the status quo cannot simply be abrogated even by a determined government. Very few believe that a solution is possible. Even though the haredim have maneuvered themselves into a corner on the public cost of their privileges, they will not yield in their implacable demand to spread the writ of halacha. Meanwhile, the influence of religious Zionism has become weaker than ever on the interpretation of this body of Jewish law and doctrine: instead, these Zionists have turned nationalist and expansionist. And in the early years of this new century, the legitimacy and charisma of the nation's political leadership fell far short of those who even at the creation of the state were forced into a tawdry compromise. It shows no more signs of dissolving now than it did sixty-five years ago when Israel was born in hope.

WHILE BEN-GURION BROUGHT THE ULTRA-ORTHODOX AGUDAT Israel into his coalition governments, he was careful to limit the significance of this partnership. The number of religious seminary students who were granted exemption from army service did not exceed several hundred, and their support imposed a marginal burden on the government's budget. Also, the Agudat Israel school system received only partial support, and in those days it was teaching core subjects like English mathematics and science apart from Talmud lessons, which thoroughly dominate the curriculum of all ultra-Orthodox schools today.

It was only when Israel's first right-wing coalition government took office in 1977 that the partnership with the ultra-Orthodox gained a special significance. The victory of Begin's Likud Party came as a surprise even to him after twenty-nine years in the political wilderness. Even so, thanks to the Israeli system of proportional representation, Likud did not elect enough members of the Knesset to form a government on its own. At first Begin sought the support of a newly established centrist party headed by the celebrated archeologist-general Yigal Yadin, but too many of his party in the Knesset preferred to link up with Labor and thus deny power to Begin.

So Begin turned to the haredim. He promised to continue their military exemption and expand the subsidies to their yeshivot, even though these concessions ran counter to his own secular Zionism and his personal history as commander of the Irgun forces during the fight for independence. From the haredi members he got nothing in return except their support, and even for that he had to haggle with them. The legacy of this political deal was the breakdown of Israel's national consensus and the creation of a social framework in which a majority works and serves, and a minority does neither.

4

What Is the Law
of Israel?

T HE LAW OF THE STATE OF ISRAEL IS NOT THE TEN COM-
mandments engraved on stone tablets that were given to
Moses on Mount Sinai. Nor is it the elaborate halacha that
evolved through debates by the Hebrew sages over the centuries
to set the bounds of Jewish life in the Diaspora after the destruction of the Temple. As a modern state, Israel has developed its
unique body of law based on its Ottoman inheritance and the
great body of British common law that evolved over centuries in
a homogeneous society that operates on social consensus. What
the newly formed and contentious State of Israel does not have
is a written constitution like that of the United States of America and many modern European nations.

In practical terms, the founding document of the State of Is-
rael is the 1947 UN General Assembly resolution. It called for the
creation of a Jewish state and an Arab state in the territory of
Palestine, lying between the Mediterranean Sea and the Jordan
River, and clearly followed the policies of the secular majority:
"The preparatory assembly of each [Jewish and Arab] state shall

create a democratic constitution for the country." This did not mean a state organized on religious lines, and the founders of Israel took this seriously—even the armed Jewish nationalists who were ready to fight for a state that extended to the Jordan and possibly beyond. According to the 1948 proclamation establishing the State of Israel on May 15, "We declare that, from the moment of the end of the [British] Mandate tonight until the setting up of elected and orderly bodies of the State in accordance with the constitution to be created by the preparatory assembly no later than October 1, 1948, the Council of the People shall operate as the temporary Council of State."

But Israel's actual founding document turned out to be its Declaration of Independence, a pastiche of ideological compromises cobbled together and amended in four days as a bitter war broke out against Arab troops who had invaded the partitioned land. The Declaration bears little trace of either messianic fervor or hatred for the enemy; it resounds with pathos for the millions lost in the Holocaust, and its overriding themes are secular. Observant Jews never use the word for God, but the Almighty is not even mentioned in any traditional euphemism, only implied in the phrase "the Rock of Israel."

What happened afterward can be seen as bitter disappointment for a people who literally invented the idea of law through the Ten Commandments as the foundation of its identity. Because of the divide between those who want a state for Jews and those who want a Jewish state, after more than sixty years, the State of Israel still does not have a founding law—a constitution. The principal reason for this failure is the opposition of religious elements, which argue from their unshakeable belief that Israel already *has* a religious law—given to Moses on Mount Sinai—and therefore has no need for a constitution. They know that it would contain

On May 15, 1948, David Ben-Gurion and members of his temporary government met at the hall of the then-Tel Aviv Museum to read the hastingly signed Declaration of Independence, in which the equality of women and a permanent constitution were promised but never fulfilled.

clauses bringing law into line with that of a modern state, for example, granting rights to women that most likely would differ from more restrictive religious law. At first Israel's lawmakers did not see the seriousness of this problem. After all, halacha had already evolved over the centuries, and today no one would suggest that a man be executed because of homosexuality, as the Bible decrees in Leviticus 20:13: "Two men caught performing anal intercourse should both be put to death." Likewise, the attitude toward women has changed since the time of the Torah; a thousand years ago Jewish communities in Europe banned polygamy although it represented a change in the halacha.

The failure to adopt a constitution represented a political victory by the ultra-Orthodox minority in its struggle to maintain the upper hand over the secular majority because it helps maintain the halacha as a static body of law in defiance of Jewish tradition of argument and interpretation. Even the etymology of the word *halacha* goes against them: as interpreted by many scholars, it derives from the Hebrew root *haloch*, which means "to walk." Thus, it is unlike the Muslim law of sharia—meaning the set path remaining frozen as it evolves from the Koran in the seventh century. Jewish religious law, although given to Moses on Mount Sinai, has evolved as the life of the Jewish people changed. But even that evolution of the law is rooted in intellectual debate and theological interpretation that has not been a defining feature of Muslim societies. With the democratic awakening of the Arab Spring, that could be about to change. But just as in Israel, political groups are emerging that define themselves by a more or less strict interpretation of religious law, its relation to civil law, and even among Muslim as well as Jewish fundamentalists, whether civil law should exist at all.

Consider the Mishna, created by Jewish sages in Israel during the first three centuries of the Christian era, after the Romans destroyed Jerusalem's Second Temple and ended Jewish rule in the land known in Latin as Palestina. Without self-rule and priestly guidance, the Jews needed to clarify the mitzvoth—the laws and rules for the conduct of life that bind Jews together. This codification attempted to not only maintain the ancient law practiced by the Jewish priests but adapt it to the contemporary needs of a people in crisis. The Talmud, a massive creation by disputatious scholars and rabbis from the fifth to the seventh centuries, interpreted and elaborated on the rules of the Mishna. Indeed, there are two versions of the Talmud, one attributed to the sages of Jerusalem and the other to those in Babylon (in modern-day Iraq), further evidence of the continuing task of adjusting ancient law to local culture. Lest they be accused of undermining a foreign ruler, these scholars adopted as a rule the Aramaic saying *dina demalchuta dina*—the law of the kingdom is our law.

The early settlers in Palestine accepted first Ottoman and then British law. The haphazardly drawn status quo agreement of 1947 envisioned a separation between halacha and civil law as the basis for constitutional discussions about relations between state and synagogue. The Yishuv's leaders viewed it as no more than a commitment by the Jews of modern Palestine to take into account the interests of the Orthodox in the new state. So it came as a shock when the haredim sought to make halacha the law of the land, and Ben-Gurion abandoned the idea of a constitution.

In the first decade of statehood, the founders adhered to the agreement, which dated back only to the 1930s and the rule of the British. Changes were demanded by many, including one future prime minister then known as Goldie Meyerson, a political force in Israel's labor movement and a signer of its Declaration of Independence. But these changes were put aside for the constitution that was supposedly in the making.

Benjamin Akzin, a political scientist at the Hebrew University in Jerusalem, likened a constitution to a lock on a door preventing strangers and enemies from entering the place and destroying it. The lock could always be broken, he explained, and determined people could even gain entrance by knocking down a wall, but this requires time and effort, so the lock fulfills its function against intruders. It is simpler for the owners—the citizens of a democratic country—to rearrange the furniture to accommodate changing tenants. Thus he compared an existing system of laws to the furniture that is shifted by succeeding tenants, who nevertheless find it much more difficult to remodel the basic structure of the house.

Ben-Gurion and his supporters did not at first foresee any difficulty in adopting a written constitution in the American manner. And if in America it was felt necessary to establish and equip the building with a strong lock, the founders of Israel—whose inhabitants also came from many countries without a democratic tradition—also wanted to construct a solid legal framework. Even before the state was established, Dr. Leo Kohn, a distinguished legal scholar and a member of the Jewish Agency, was instructed to prepare a draft. Once the state was established, a government-appointed committee headed by Zerah Warhaftig, a lawyer of the National Religious Party and a rabbi, was given the task of working from Kohn's proposals. Warhaftig, who was inclined to introduce many elements of halacha, saw no contradiction between his views and those who believed in the supremacy of the future constitution. At the same time, representatives of Agudat Israel entered the discussions, and a dispute immediately arose over the status quo agreement. It has never really subsided, marked by protest movements and demonstrations demanding a constitution. The essence of the dispute has always been whether the final authority over the meaning and application of the law would lie with the Supreme Court or the rabbinate. Although there were several reasons behind the Israeli religious establishment's objection to a secular constitution, the most forceful, although the one cited least because of its discriminatory odor, was that a constitutional guarantee of equal rights for women would contradict Jewish tradition.

Among the many suggestions that attracted public support was a draft by law professors from Tel Aviv University, headed by Professor Uriel Reichman. It would have allowed citizens to choose between religious or civil marriage ceremonies and a religious or secular burial. It would have revoked the ban on raising pigs and the marketing of pork products, and permitted the public display of food that would otherwise be forbidden during Passover week—most notably bread. The legal scholars also recommended direct election of at least half of the members of the Knesset (still chosen only from party lists on the basis of proportional representation), and setting a minimum number of votes for any party to be represented in the Knesset at 2.5 percent of all voters. One of the reasons for the rejection of the professors' proposal was the secular majority's reluctance to provoke an open conflict with the haredim, who would have been severely disadvantaged by a system favoring mainstream over single-issue parties.

Pragmatist that he was, Ben-Gurion soon lost interest in a written constitution and realized that Israel could function without one, which it has done, with the likelihood of a comprehensive document receding as the coercive power of the religious minority has increased. The ultra-Orthodox remained faithful to the idea of a religious state eventually ruled by a Messiah. One reason was an early political marker laid down by secularists who refused to declare Judaism the official religion of the country, overriding the objections of some of the haredim and establishing that halacha would not be part of the state's legal foundation.

With the constitutional debate gridlocked over principle, the political leaders of the new state decided to sidestep the opposition by adopting a series of Basic Laws. Over the years, the Knesset adopted a number of these laws, which differ from ordinary legislation only in the stipulation that they could be amended by a firmer majority—more than half the members of the Knesset instead of merely half of those present and voting. It has not proven difficult to mobilize 61 of the 120 members of the Knesset on a single issue, so that the Basic Laws do not have the permanence of a constitution. By March 1997 the Knesset had approved eleven Basic Laws that were designed as the basis for a constitution. Most dealt with noncontroversial topics, such as the president of the state, the armed forces, and the state controller. In the 1990s two more Basic Laws were adopted that only hint indirectly at the controversy between the ultras and the secular majority: one guarantees citizens the freedom to pursue an occupation of their choice; another deals with human dignity and individual rights.

Several clauses of these essentially tolerant statutes aroused controversy and were either changed or deleted because of vehement opposition by the religious parties. The law covering freedom of work stipulated that a citizen or resident of Israel is "entitled to pursue any occupation or profession he wishes." The ultras protested that this could be interpreted as allowing any Israeli to import nonkosher food, and this was quickly dropped. The opening paragraph of the civil rights law was attacked by the religious parties even though it was based on what seemed to be an innocuous passage in the Declaration of Independence that declared: "The rights of man in the State of Israel, based on the value of man, the sacredness of his life, and his being free, are to be honored in the spirit of the principles of the Declaration."

Not surprisingly, there is no Basic Law guaranteeing equal rights, lest it undermine the authority of the rabbinical courts, where women cannot serve as judges or, in some haredi courts, even be accepted as witnesses. In June 2010, after a ten-year delay, Israel's Supreme Court used the Law of the Budget to declare stipends to yeshiva students illegal on the ground that they discriminate against students in secular institutions of higher education, whose state grants had been canceled in the year 2000 as an economic measure. The budget legislation directs the government to provide monetary support on an equal basis, but it is not a Basic Law. The court nevertheless left the haredim in shock by ruling that all students are equal, which means that a significant proportion of their income would be eliminated in the following year's budget despite threats of massive protests. One possible solution would be to restore the stipend to other students, thus enabling the grants to yeshiva students to continue. But university attendance has expanded in recent years as Israel has become a knowledge-based economy, and the burden of supporting them would weigh too heavily on the Treasury.

One Basic Law, urgently needed but blocked by the religious parties, would stipulate the predominance of the civil courts over the rabbinical courts. Even under Ottoman rule over Palestine, when the religious courts originated, their power was clearly limited to questions of personal status such as marriage, divorce, and burial. Only in rare cases did the religious courts enter into borderline areas like marital disputes over inheritance. The lack of legislation clearly defining the jurisdiction of the rabbinical courts of course arises from constant efforts by the haredi parties to restrain the power of the civil courts and especially that of the Supreme Court, whose growing influence they recognize as the gravest threat to their campaign to override civil law and impose halacha on the State of Israel. Dr. Ya'akov Ne'eman, the minister of justice in Netanyahu's second government, once made a speech suggesting that financial disputes might be judged according to the rules of the rabbinical court. He quickly backed away from the idea, which created such an uproar in Israel that it was never mentioned in public again.

5

Who Enforces
the Law?

Y A'AKOV NE'EMAN IS ONE OF ISRAEL'S MOST DISTIN-
guished public servants—a lawyer and educator who was
named minister of justice without even first being elected
to parliament. At a conference of rabbis in 2009, he suggested that
the Bible contains "a complete solution to all the things we are
dealing with" and made a startling proposal that "Torah law must
be the law of the State of Israel." He might as well have set off a
bomb in a courtroom. It made little difference that he said religious law would replace civil law only gradually, or that he tried
to back away from his remarks the next day by explaining that he
only wanted to consult Torah law when proposed legislation had
no civil precedent. It also did little to soften the words of this
observant Jew when he argued that rabbinical courts could lighten
the load on the civil justice system by acting as mediators in matrimonial disputes over alimony.

Even those inclined to forgive him because of his eminence
agreed with a retired Supreme Court justice, Dalia Dorner, who
said that justice ministers should be more careful in expressing

their own heart's desire, even if they did not intend to replace the laws of the state with the religious law of halacha. The question was not so much the law itself but who would write it: the democratically elected members of the Knesset or the rabbis as representatives of divine law? In Israel, established as a secular state and homeland for Jews whether observant or not, parliament makes the laws; the government carries them out; and the judicial system acts as critic and coordinator. But the anger aroused among Israel's secular majority was only intensified by the widespread resentment that the Knesset had already ceded deeply personal questions such as marriage and divorce to the oversight and interpretation of religious courts.

What should have alerted Ne'eman to choose his words more carefully was the constant friction between the civil judiciary and religious groups that do not accept its independence and barely its writ. Indeed, the makers of Israel's laws already are beholden to the religious parties; they wield a kind of veto by their role in any coalition government. One of their abiding goals is to broaden the limited authority of the rabbinical courts, and many of the ultras would prefer to submit all civil disputes to rabbinical authority, which admits no women judges and which limits even the appearance of women as witnesses.

Zionism never advocated a complete separation between religion and the state. The movement's religious wing was a significant part of the Jewish revival and tried to link the building of a new land to the traditions of the past. Although the ultra-Orthodox adherents of Agudat Israel waged a relentless rearguard action against the reality of a modern state with an ancient past, in the end they had to yield to it. One spokesman for the ultras, Rabbi Moshe Akiva Druk, actually proposed resolving the dilemma by giving religious courts jurisdiction over all financial matters. In fact, civil disputes over property, money, and associated economic questions can be litigated before civilian judges—even property settlements in divorce cases despite the rabbis' insistence that they have jurisdiction.

The secular majority rejected the rabbis by adopting the civil law inherited from the British mandate and thus followed Zionism's founder, Theodor Herzl, who envisioned a "state for Jews" and not "a Jewish state." Israel's Supreme Court, the highest authority in civil disputes, can also act as a court to resolve disputes over fundamental principles of law and governance by sitting as a *bagatz*—the Hebrew acronym for "Supreme Court of Justice."

The ultra-Orthodox community has not accepted this role for the court, demonstrating against it but never challenging it before the law. Instead they tend to circumvent civil courts and seek arbitration by unauthorized authorities, leading to serious conundrums after religious courts order settlements contradicting Israeli law in cases of tax evasion, bribery, or financial fraud. What happens to a complaint against a rabbinical court justice accused of accepting a bribe to correct what appears to be a legal error? In most cases civil court judges are reluctant to invoke supremacy, but early in 2011 the attorney general convinced Ne'eman as justice minister to take action against Rabbi Dov Domb, head of the rabbinical court in Petach Tikva. The rabbi was accused of accepting a bribe to end the marriage of a retarded couple whom he had wed six months earlier. The money was paid by the father of the groom, and the facts of the case were not disputed. In 2012, at the initiative of two religious members, the Knesset adopted a law that would enable the civil court to impose sanctions on members of a rabbinical court that neglects to impose sanctions on husbands who evade granting a divorce that was ordered by the rabbinical court.

Attempts to sidestep Israeli civil law have become a tactic of the haredim in their constant attempts to undermine the authority of state courts and especially the Supreme Court. The chief target of the haredim was former chief justice Aharon Barak. When he headed the court between 1996 and 2006, Barak argued that "every dispute can be examined by a court of justice." What he meant by that was that the high court had the right to address any dispute, civil or criminal. His bold interpretations extended to striking down Knesset legislation if, according to the Supreme Court, it contradicted existing law. By following the lead of the U.S. Supreme Court, this erudite jurist bridged the legal gap that existed in Israel, where political gridlock with the ultra-Orthodox has blocked the adoption of a written constitution.

The ultra-Orthodox were angered by complex decisions that tended to legitimize the financial implications of same-sex couples and Reform Jewish conversions made abroad, and to reconsider the Sabbath closing of Jerusalem's Bar-Ilan Road. The fight reached its peak in 1998 when the court ruled illegal the arrangement to defer and in effect exempt yeshiva students from military service. In the case of the Bar-Ilan Road, the ultras picked the wrong target in Justice Barak, who had actually sought a compromise. The road connects the Ramat Eshkol neighborhood and the northern exit from the city, and the haredim wanted it closed all day on the Sabbath because the road goes through a religious neighborhood. Barak proposed closing it only during the hours of religious services, while other high court jurists opposed closing any roads at all.

Menachem Porush, the leader of Agudat Israel, succeeded in uniting all haredi factions in a mass demonstration demanding that the Supreme Court change its pluralistic views of religion and the state. The demonstration, which even drew supporters of

Agudat Israel's rival Shas Party, took place in front of the Knesset in Jerusalem on February 14, 1999, and followed a series of personal attacks on the judges. The haredim claimed an attendance of 250,000 although the "enemy media" estimated the turnout at far less. The leaders delivered fiery speeches in Hebrew and Yiddish and blew the traditional ram's horn. One of the placards read, THE TORAH OF ISRAEL CANNOT BE JUDGED—a slogan that condenses the essence of the dispute between the secular majority and the haredi minority by asserting that civil law cannot override the religious commandments of the Bible. By extension, it also claims that civil judges interpreting the laws of the Knesset are inferior to the interpretations of the rabbis on how the state and its citizens should conduct their lives. Even for a "Jewish state" this is a breathtaking claim of authority.

One of the most inflammatory attackers was Rabbi Ovadia Yosef, the Shas leader known for his vitriolic rhetoric. He accused the Supreme Court judges of not believing in either the written or oral Torah. "Who are these people?" he cried. "Empty headed ignoramuses. They don't know how to read a single mishna [the founding codifications of Jewish legal tradition]; they know less than one of our seven-year-old children. They call themselves a Supreme Court, but they aren't even the equals of the lowest of courts."

Meanwhile, Rabbi Ya'akov Aryeh Alter, who carries the title of Admor—an honorific for a Hasidic rabbi—met several times with Netanyahu, who was then leader of the opposition, and petitioned him to abandon the current method of choosing the Supreme Court. Instead of the justices being nominated by a committee of judges, lawyers, and government ministers, he favored the politicized American method of nomination by the president and confirmation by the Senate. Netanyahu replied that it was too late to change the long-standing Israeli system, but as the 1999 parliamentary elections approached, Netanyahu made an agreement with Porush of Agudat Israel to establish a committee of legal authorities—including some haredim—to investigate limiting the Supreme Court's authority through legislation. The haredim then moderated their attacks lest they hurt Netanyahu's campaign, but Ehud Barak's Labor Party swamped Netanyahu's Likud at the polls, and that ended his deal with Porush.

Nevertheless, an informal tradition took root over the years to apportion representation among the eleven members of the Supreme Court as vacancies occurred when judges retired at the mandatory age of seventy. At least one of the eleven judges now is an observant follower of religious tradition, although not formally a representative of a religious party. (One judge also must be an Arab and two must be women.) The nominating committee remains an independent body and has been praised both in Israel and abroad for its professionalism. Its nominees are routinely confirmed by Israel's president, and although they are not always free of political taint, they display far less political bias than the nine judges of America's highest court.

The committee also changed its procedures by deciding that any nominee would have to receive the support of seven of the nine committee members. While this could limit the prospects of controversial although capable candidates, it also makes outright political appointments and deals more difficult and strengthens the court's independence and stature in the long run. When three judges were appointed to fill empty seats on the Supreme Court in 2009, there was almost no public controversy.

But despite the success in repelling the attacks of the haredim, many lawyers feel that the Supreme Court and the entire judicial system have paid a high price. Fearful of criticism, judges are more cautious in confronting attacks by the haredim and political extremists. One prominent lawyer, who insists on anonymity lest he fall afoul of the judges themselves, confides: "The Supreme Court has begun to censor itself. Even when its authority is not in doubt, it is not sure that the government, as the executive power, will give the proper backing to its decisions."

Consider the court's cautious and reluctant criticism when the government was accused of violating its own laws in erecting the wall separating Israel from territories of the West Bank. It also has been less than severe in cases dealing with the haredim, especially the yeshiva students' exemption from military service. Many have forgotten that this is not a right embedded in law but in a political agreement backed only by the force of tradition. After the Israeli Supreme Court under Chief Justice Aharon Barak ruled that the government had no legal right to grant the exemption, a committee was formed to define limited terms of military service for yeshiva students. But even after these were enacted into law neither the government nor the Supreme Court dared to enforce them and kept extending the deadline to work out a solution with the ultra-Orthodox leaders.

In 2007, Prime Minister Ehud Olmert appointed as his justice minister Daniel Friedman, a distinguished law professor who had favored the reform of selecting judges, leading the haredim to hope that the Supreme Court would be weakened and the government would become more amenable to the ultras' pressure. But Friedman was not reappointed when Olmert was forced to resign in a scandal and was succeeded by Netanyahu. Friedman's successor, Ya'akov Ne'eman, took a more theoretical but politically adept approach in questioning civil over religious authority, making his comments on Torah law and then quickly backing away from them. But he supported a religious candidate as attorney general and even pressured the government and Knesset to divide the work of the attorney general between two officials— one to act as the government's legal adviser and the other to run the government's prosecution service. Even though Friedman couched his proposal in professional terms, it was likely to weaken the judicial system and was opposed by most former Supreme Court justices.

This dispute has gone on for years: is the attorney general a legal adviser to the government in the widest sense of the term, or merely a lawyer whose job is to defend it? Attempts have been made to learn from the experience of other democracies that have separated these two legal roles (like Britain) or combined them (like the United States). Although such a technical argument does not seem to have any bearing on the struggle between the ultras and the secular public, there is great uneasiness lest a division of legal authority strengthen the haredim, who fear a strong attorney general with powers broad enough to enforce judicial decisions. Behind this is the hidden agenda of the religious parties who see a separate public prosecutor carrying less authority in the struggle between civil and religious courts for legal supremacy.

The religious parties' campaign against the civil judiciary received another setback in the selection of a successor to the outgoing attorney general, Manny Mazuz. The public committee charged with selecting a successor managed to deflect the influence of politicians, including Ne'eman. Neither of the two religious candidates he backed was accepted, and Ne'eman had no alternative but to agree to the unanimous nomination of Yehuda Weinstein, a noted criminal lawyer and former prosecutor. He is seen as a relatively neutral figure, but the dispute is nevertheless likely to continue as long as the divisions persist over the role of religion in the Israeli state and society.

The dispute is rooted in the argument over whether Israel should be a Jewish state or merely a state for the Jewish people. This distinction is bewildering to friends and enemies everywhere but should not be. These opposing concepts are often veiled by technical arguments such as the one about the powers of the attorney general; then they break into the open. Another argument literally burst into flame in 2011 at the start of Israel's anniversary celebrations. A Chabad rabbi, chosen for the honor of lighting one of the twelve celebratory bonfires, changed the traditional call—"In honor of the State of Israel"—to "In honor of the State of *Eretz* Israel." This not only was a clear deviation from the nation's official name but invoked a partisan political slogan. Eretz Israel refers to the biblical borders of what is known in song and story as the Promised Land. It includes what is now the West Bank, the area claimed by Palestinians as their own but occupied by Israel since 1967.

No question in Israeli politics or diplomacy is more deeply influenced by Jewish history, tradition, and religion than this, although these aspects are so fundamental that they seem beyond solution, and the future of the West Bank is mainly discussed in terms of Israel's security and its role in the defense against Arab attack. And so it is with other, more mundane disputes ranging from education to divorce: What are the foundations and laws of Zion? What are the organizing principles of the Israeli state and how shall the Jews there shape their lives?

6

What Should You
Teach Your Son?

BEIT SHEMESH (THE HOUSE OF THE SUN) IS A THRIVING industrial town on the western slopes of the Hills of Judea, built sixty years ago on the site of an ancient town to absorb some of the mass of immigrants who swarmed into Israel during the first years of the state. In biblical times it was the place where the heroic Samson killed an attacking lion with the jawbone of an ass as his only weapon. His legendary strength was a divine gift to save the Israelites from the invasion of the Philistines from their coastal stronghold in Gaza. He abstained from wine but not from women and so was captured by the charms of Delilah, who cut his hair and thus robbed him of magical power.

Today, Beit Shemesh seems to have heroes who display more strength. Although they are ultra-Orthodox haredim, they have heroically stood against their own community in their determination to provide their sons with the educational tools to secure their future, preparing the religious students to provide for themselves and their families when they grow to adulthood. In a town ruled by a municipal council where the Orthodox have a firm majority, a group of American haredi settlers have helped to build an educational system unlike most haredi schools by introducing a curriculum that includes all core subjects—English, the Hebrew language, history, science, arts, and physical education as well as a heavy schedule of Jewish studies. Their sharpest critics in Beit Shemesh are not the minority of secular inhabitants of the town but the more extreme orthodox, Neturei Karta, who object to any compromise to what they see as life in accordance with the halacha.

Rabbi Daniel Simon, the principal of the Magen Avot (Shield of Our Fathers) school in the heart of these extremists— including those who did not hesitate to spit in public on a nine-year-old girl because they did not like the way she was dressed—is proud of the achievements of the one thousand boys between the ages of six and fourteen in his school, in their academic courses as well as in Jewish studies. Many of the parents are immigrants from the United States and insist on giving their children an education similar to their own, which equipped them for life and work in the modern world. Moreover, girls are not raised to be kept in the kitchen barefoot and pregnant. The Magen Avot school for girls is headed by Rabbi Simon's wife, Dvora. The sexes are separate, but both schools teach core subjects.

Rabbi Simon is a native of the Far Rockaway neighborhood of New York City and holds a master's degree in business administration from Baltimore University. Lest he provoke the local haredi establishment, he carefully avoids emphasizing how special Magen Avot is. He merely notes that during Israel's first decades there were several haredi schools where core subjects were part of the curriculum, but their number and influence gradually waned. One of the last such schools in Ramat Gan was forced to close several years ago as a result of the gradual swing toward a more extreme form of orthodoxy.

Indeed, during the first years of the new state there were three distinct systems, all supported by the government: a generalized system of secular schools, a religious system largely influenced by religious Zionists, and an independent system that emphasized Jewish studies but—like Magen Avot—taught basic language and mathematical skills and history. Only in later years, as the political influence of the haredim grew, did a fourth system of education gain momentum. Ultra-Orthodox schools for children under the age of fourteen offered Jewish subjects almost exclusively. The success of the school in Beit Shemesh is a sign that the pendulum can also swing back.

Rabbi Simon, an elegantly bearded man in his forties who is equally fluent in Hebrew and English, says Israeli government financing covers about 70 percent of the school's budget; for the rest he depends on what he calls "outside sources," apparently contributions from Israel and abroad. He says that schools founded by the Shas movement have begun to extend their curriculum beyond religious instruction and include core subjects. There is also a yeshiva for older boys between the ages of fourteen and eighteen, which continues the mixed curriculum of the younger school for about twenty students, many American-born. The school is located in the moshav—a cooperative village—of Zanoach, which borders Beit Shemesh. Why Zanoach and not Beit Shemesh itself? Apparently the founders of the new yeshiva were careful not to antagonize the Beit Shemesh municipality, still dominated by the old-line haredim.

But the ultra-Orthodox had no intention of yielding control over the form and content of education inside city limits. Just before the beginning of the school year in September 2011, fifteen hard-line yeshiva students burst into the compound of a new girls' school offering core subjects in the state's religious system. The youthful invaders claimed that they objected to seeing so many "females" close to their homes, prompting the haredi mayor of Beit Shemesh, Moshe Abutbul, to intervene. He argued for "compromise" on the status of the school, but the angry parents stood firm on the rights of their neighborhood and demanded that the invaders leave. The dispute drew public attention almost immediately. The Ministry of Education and even the prime minister's office intervened on the side of the parents, and the yeshiva students were evicted by the police.

In most countries it would be impossible for schools to offer a curriculum composed only of religious studies. (There is one known exception in the United States, Kiryas Joel, in Rockland County, about thirty miles north of New York City. The community is led by the extreme Satmar Hasidim. Their leaders trade the community's bloc vote in elections for what amounts to exemptions from educational standards in state-funded schools and even from police oversight of questionable behavior by this strict cult. The Orthodox voters have gained control of the local school board although their children attend religious schools by a ratio of more than two to one over the eight thousand public school students. In 2012, residents sued to remove five Orthodox board members, accusing them of diverting state funds to the private Jewish schools for transportation, books, and special education.)

In England, a group of Jews belonging to the Beltz Hasidim —named after a Polish town where the group was founded in the eighteenth century—came into conflict with the law when they founded a strictly religious school. It was called Talmud Torah Mahzikei Hadas (Preservers of Religion), and the Beltz founders argued that since they did not seek or accept government funding, they could eliminate subjects required by British law in order to concentrate on religious studies. As reported by the Israeli

The main study hall of Mir Yeshiva in Meah She'arim, one of the centers of the ultra-Orthodox in Jerusalem

author Moshe Pearl, the British Ministry of Education almost immediately issued a ruling against the school's Board of Guardians. When the case went to court, the civil judges ruled that the Ministry of Education had a right to oversee the Hasidic school's curriculum because its graduates, like all other British schoolchildren, must be trained in languages, mathematics, and other subjects they would need to hold a job and not become a burden on society. In the Netherlands the government demanded that a Roman Catholic school operated mostly with public funds offer a broad general curriculum similar to that in all other Dutch schools, religious or secular.

In the Holy Land, the controversy has long played out between those who favor a single track of education restricted to

Talmudic studies, and those who are in favor of combining these studies with a general education. It began more than a hundred years ago when, just as in the Jewish bastions of Eastern Europe, only the very few brightest students devoted themselves to full-time yeshiva study of the Talmud. The Old Yishuv (as the Orthodox were called when Palestine was under foreign rule) were the absolute majority, and all boys were expected to go to primary school—commonly called *cheder*—where mainly the Hebrew language, religious ritual, and the early books of the Bible were taught. (This concentration on Jewish studies would violate the current education laws of the State of Israel; girls were most often exempt from any studies at all, and this now is also illegal.) Late in the nineteenth century, the Jewish charitable organizations in each major country opened schools of their own, mainly in Jerusalem, to offer a basic education as well as teach traditional Jewish studies. These foundations established the schools with a dual purpose: to help advance their poor brethren in their ancient homeland, but also to block the spread of Christian missionary schools among both the Arab and Jewish youth.

These organizations included the German Deutsche Hilfsverein, the French Alliance Israelite, and the English Evelyn de Rothschild Foundation. Each school emphasized the language of its donor country. Not everybody in the Old Yishuv welcomed these modern schools, and many insisted on giving their sons a traditional Talmudic education in religious schools. But others were more tolerant, like the family of Professor Yosef Yoel Rivlin, the father of Reuven Rivlin, speaker of the Knesset since 2009. The Rivlin family were among the students of the Vilna Gaon who immigrated to Palestine early in the nineteenth century. Yosef Yoel Rivlin studied in Jerusalem in the Lemel School established by the German Hilfsverein. It also sent him to Germany, where he earned a doctorate in philology, specializing in Arabic. Professor Rivlin later became the first modern scholar to translate the Koran into Hebrew. The Hilfsverein also laid the foundation for a technical college in Haifa that soon became the Technion, Israel's first engineering school and now world famous as a scientific center of research and teaching. Courses were expected to be taught in German, since its founders could not conceive that Hebrew could provide the terminology needed for its technical curriculum. But modern Hebrew proved highly adaptable, and the use of German became literally verboten for political reasons; now the scientists and their students work in Hebrew and English and have links with many foreign centers of higher learning. Also during the early years of the last century, the Alliance Israelite of French Jewry established the Kiach—acronym of the school system of Kol Israel Chaverim (Alliance Israelite)—and British Jews set up the Rothschild school in Jerusalem, which was widely known by the name of its longtime principal, Miss Annie Landau.

The Zionist movement itself did not neglect education and in 1905 established the Gymnasia Herzliya in Tel Aviv, named after the Zionist founder Theodor Herzl. This was the first modern secondary school for boys and girls between the ages of six and eighteen and was soon followed by several other secular schools, including the Gymnasia Ivrit in Jerusalem and the Reali School in Haifa. Hebrew was studied as a living language not as a sacred vehicle; it was the language of instruction and the language commonly used by students among themselves. The founders of all these schools aimed to revitalize ancient Jewish culture, and to them the creation of a living Hebrew language was no less important than the Zionist pioneers' return to the soil—and they succeeded in their aims through the schools.

When the state was established in 1948, Ben-Gurion's policy was to unite all schools under one system offering equal and free education to all children. Regardless of their origin or curriculum, all schools were merged into one system, which nevertheless offered parents a choice between those with either a secular or a religious emphasis. To allow for specialization, the law also permitted each school to add to the basic required curriculum courses in one-quarter of the subjects according to local choice. This loophole gave impetus to the establishment of a number of schools that provide an enrichment program in accordance with the educational system of the Reform and Conservative synagogues. (These variants of Jewish observance exist in Israel, but they are not widespread, and they lack the political and social power of the Orthodox that was granted by the status quo agreement.) Thus the educational system of the new state was designed to fulfill the basic educational requirements common to advanced countries, but pressure by the ultra-Orthodox parties soon produced a third classification known as Hinuch Atzmai (Independent Education), which quickly evolved into a strict religious school system that avoided the study of basic subjects altogether.

These schools now dominate the haredi educational system, creating an ever-widening gap between the ultra-Orthodox minority and the rest of Israeli society. Perhaps the most tragic aspect of this review of Israeli education is that the Magen Avot school in Beit Shemesh is an exception to the trend. The most urgent problem created by the separation of the ultras is the continuing reduction of haredim in Israel's labor force. Government statistics record that the proportion of haredi pupils in Israeli schools doubled from 6 percent in 1960 to 12 percent in 2000, and is projected by the Central Bureau of Statistics to reach 14 percent in 2014. In 2010, for the first time more than half of the class entering primary school in Jerusalem were haredi children.

Beit Shalom Yeshiva, associated with Mir Yeshiva in Meah She'arim

The simple explanation of this rapid increase is the very high birthrate of the haredi community.

The gradual elimination of core studies in haredi schools has become the main subject of friction between several Israeli governments and the ultra-Orthodox parties. The dispute centers not on what they teach in their schools and seminaries but on what they do *not* teach. These places of learning undermine Israeli society not only by producing graduates largely unable to find gainful employment but also by breaking the law that requires that all schools be inspected by the Ministry of Education to ensure they are following the approved curriculum.

For years negotiations have dragged on between state educational authorities and the ultra-Orthodox educational institutions on whether and which subjects should become part of their curriculum: Hebrew language, English, mathematics, or the sciences. The fact is that the ultra-Orthodox hold all the bargaining chips in these negotiations because they are prepared to bring down any government if they are pressured to modernize and reform along the lines of secular schools. Most haredi schools simply could not fulfill the requirements of the state curriculum. Their teachers are ill-equipped to do so, and most of their schools do not have facilities for physical education. Their allocation from the Ministry of Education is usually spent providing transportation and free lunches for their pupils—two items that have become an attraction for parents to register their children. Most come from North African and other Oriental Jewish communities, and free buses and free lunch are often more important to their parents than the long-range quality of the education.

While these haredi schools obviously operate outside the law, no Israeli prime minister has been ready to risk his coalition in order to apply it. In 2008, after arduous negotiations, Yuli Tamir, minister of education in the government headed by Ehud Olmert, succeeded in reaching what was hailed as a compromise agreement with the ultra-Orthodox political parties for the haredi schools to teach core subjects up to the age of fourteen. But both sides knew that these were empty words; the schools had neither the intention nor the money to adopt a modern curriculum.

Once the government allocation is spent on food and transportation, there is not enough money left for qualified teachers of core subjects. Most of the poorly paid teachers of Jewish law and ritual are not qualified to teach English and mathematics. In any case, the inspectors from the Ministry of Education are usually prevented from actually inspecting haredi schools. If they do, the inspectors are often accused of political intervention, a charge that, if pressed, could destabilize any government. Two years after the supposed agreement to modernize the curriculum, two distinguished lawyers attacked the compromise in court as a sham. Amnon Rubinstein, a former minister of education, and Professor Uriel Reichman, president of the Herzliya Interdisciplinary Center, filed suit on behalf of four former students of Orthodox schools, alleging that inadequate instruction had thwarted their hopes of following professional careers. The suit demanded that the education ministry act against the haredi school system for failing to fulfill the educational commitment made in exchange for the subsidies paid to their schools. General Elazar Stern, former chief of manpower in the Israeli army and himself a religious Jew, joined the suit, which was elevated directly to the Supreme Court.

The ultra-Orthodox reaction was emphatic and dismissive. Rabbi Shlomo Briliant, director of the association of haredi schools, told a reporter for the daily *Ha'aretz*: "All this group wants is publicity. What a Jewish boy needs to learn is Judaism. He can learn secular studies later in preparatory classes for academic education and enter any Orthodox academic seminary. Democracy means that every parent should have the right to decide what his son should learn." *Ha'aretz* columnist Na'ama

Sheffi turned the argument of the ultra-Orthodox against them. She argued that if curriculum decisions for her son were to be left up to her, then it would be fair to leave such personal decisions up to every minority, including what kind of rabbi— Orthodox, Reform, or Conservative—would be permitted to perform weddings. Likewise, she suggested that public transportation should also be available on the Sabbath for those who want to use it.

Israel's secular majority, supported by the then-largest opposition party, Kadima, supported the appeal to teach core subjects in all schools, but unless the Supreme Court orders a change in the curriculum in no uncertain terms, any government led by Netanyahu would be likely to find reasons not to interfere, lest it threaten the stability of his coalition. But even if the political and legal problems posed by the haredi school system are solved, long-term economic and fiscal problems will remain. Any agreement would eliminate busing pupils and providing them free lunches in haredi schools—or force the government to provide them to all Israeli schoolchildren, an unacceptable burden on the government budget. Even the example of the Magen Avot school in Beit Shemesh does not resolve the fiscal problem, since the school depends on donors to cover almost one-third of its costs. The simplest way to supply the sums to schools that teach the core studies required by law would be to shift the sums from the haredi schools that depend on government subsidies even as they ignore the education laws, but that has proven politically impossible.

Another aspect of the haredi school system that is in urgent need of reform is its tendency to discriminate among its pupils in order to provide a more exclusive education for some of them. The first signs appeared in the 1960s when the education ministry under Zevulun Hammer of the religious Zionist Party permitted the establishment of schools with high academic standards, which generally enrolled pupils from families with an educated background, mainly of Ashkenazi (European) origin, but they were soon disbanded. Nevertheless, in 2010 a haredi school for girls in the West Bank town of Emanuel deliberately separated girls of Ashkenzai and Sephardi (Middle Eastern and North African) background, and even built a wall that separated them in the playground. The school authorities put forward a flimsy argument that they offered two separate types of education. The case reached Israeli's Supreme Court, which ordered the parents to end the separation, but the parents refused to do so and were jailed for contempt of court. The case ended several months later in a far-fetched compromise, soon disobeyed anyway by the Ashkenazi parents.

In May 2011, the government prepared a draft law that would have made it illegal to register pupils in school on the basis of origin, family background, and even religious observance. The draft law was based on a report by the state controller that disclosed mass discrimination on the basis of family origins in haredi schools. But the law was quickly withdrawn after vehement objections by Moshe Gafni, the haredi chairman of the Knesset's powerful finance committee. Legal discrimination as well as second-class education remain the unwritten law of the land.

Haredi legislators have always taken pride in the fact that in their schools for girls the ban on core subjects is not practiced. The girls may learn less Talmud but the same amount of English, mathematics, and science as in secular and religious Zionist schools. Some of them may think that girls are bright enough to follow the fine points of Talmudic thought, but they nevertheless concede that an Orthodox wife is often charged with supporting not only her husband's studies but their children and needs the background to engage in trade, secretarial work, and accounting.

The girls of the Beit Ya'akov school system are thus qualified to sit for the state high school matriculation examination but are prevented by their rabbis from doing so. "Our girls know more, so why should we agree to an inferior test?" says Moshe Gafni, the chairman of the finance committee of the Knesset.

But what the haredi legislators really fear is that with a state diploma in their pockets, the Beit Ya'akov graduates would slip away from the influence and control of the community and take up careers of their own in the academic or commercial world. Early in 2012, Gideon Sa'ar, the Likud minister of education, found a solution for the Beit Ya'akov graduates: offer a test by the Szold Institute—originally founded by the women's Zionist organization Hadassah but now part of the education ministry. Passing the test yields a certificate that permits matriculation to all academic institutions.

Protests by the haredi camp came swiftly. "We don't want our girls to study for the sake of studying," claimed one of rabbis. "We want our girls to accumulate knowledge for the sake of the community." Haredi politicians quoted the late Rabbi Elazar Schach, the venerated leader of the Lithuanian Orthodox: "Any study by women should be for the purpose of supporting her family. Study for the sake of knowledge only is a waste of time." What matters most to the haredi rabbis is their followers' continued submission to their authority. Keeping them out of the mainstream of Israeli life cultivates a sense of dependence that solidifies control by religious leaders and their political representatives.

But these various school systems with their different curriculums serve only to create political, cultural, and religious divisions in a country of immigrants where cohesion is essential. A growing number of Israelis are therefore pressing for more uniform schools, and a group of three hundred Tel Aviv parents have applied to the education department of the municipality to add one more school to its existing eighty that will have a unified study program. The parents, a mixture of religious and secular families, believe that an all-embracing curriculum will not only provide a higher level of education but will make their children better and more productive citizens in the modern world. A closer examination of the cloistered scholastic life of today's Israeli yeshivot, especially as compared to the life of Jewish scholars through the ages, indicates they are right.

7

Torah Without Work

THE YESHIVAT HEBRON KNESSET ISRAEL IS ONE OF JERU-salem's smaller religious seminaries. It is situated in one of the capital's relatively modern neighborhoods, Givat Mordecai, near the Israel Museum and the repository of the Dead Sea Scrolls. Its name memorializes a legendary yeshiva in the ancient town of Hebron that was abandoned in 1929, when Arab rioters slaughtered sixty-nine Jewish inhabitants, descendants of those who had settled in the nineteenth century in the ancient town of the forefathers Abraham, Isaac, and Jacob. When Israeli soldiers captured Hebron during the 1967 war, they danced in a joyous Hasidic circle at the legendary site of Abraham's tomb. So this hallowed name has been adopted by several yeshivot in Jerusalem and the Orthodox town of B'nai Brak in memory of the lamented seminary that perished with its early settlers in Palestine. The one in Givat Mordecai is called Yeshiva Ketana (Small Yeshiva) intended for younger boys.

Two colors dominate the scenery: the concrete buildings covered in white plaster and the contrasting black clothing worn by students and their teachers alike, although in summer most of the boys wear long-sleeved white shirts. About seven hundred study here, the boys starting at the age of fourteen or fifteen, just after reaching the age of puberty and confirmation as adults through their bar mitzvah ceremony. They remain for about three years, or longer if they are not married and have no family of their own. In several other yeshivot, mostly belonging to the stricter sects like Neturei Karta (Watchmen of the Town), the lingua franca is Yiddish, as are the rabbinical lectures, in order not to defame the ancient language of the Bible. In Yeshivat Hebron, as in most newer religious academies, Hebrew is mainly spoken, although often pronounced, sometimes jokingly, with a Yiddish intonation, putting the emphasis on the first syllable. The dissonance grates on the ears of secular Israelis whose Hebrew puts the stress on the last syllable of each word.

The students live at the yeshiva, are awakened at 7:00 a.m., recite morning prayers, then eat breakfast and begin their studies at nine o'clock. They take a two-hour break for lunch at 1:00 p.m., then resume studies until evening prayers and supper. Then comes a study period called Seder Shlishi (Third Order), which usually lasts until midnight.

The principal subject of this intense course of study is the Gemara—the second half of the Talmud, which is the main Jewish book of law, philosophy, and ethics written between the third and seventh centuries of the Common Era. The first period of the day is held in a large common hall called Beit Hamidrash, or the House of Studies. The boys (yeshiva *bochers* as they are sympathetically called in Yiddish) divide into groups to study and discuss each day's assigned chapter. Each student offers his own interpretation, and dispute among them on points of law and interpretation is an important part of their education. Three teachers with the title of Rosh (head) of the yeshiva move among the groups to assist in clarifying points of doctrine and sharpening the process of interpretation. It is demanding training for the intellect but also severely limiting because it turns heavily on legalistic reasoning.

Since the boys are busy until the late hours of the night there is of course no homework. During their third year, groups are permitted to devise and work on their own curriculum, which does not mean they turn to secular study. The work often includes the later books of the Bible in their Hebrew original, including the Prophets and the books of wisdom like Job and Ecclesiastes, which are not taught in any systematic way in the yeshiva. The first five books of the Bible, the Torah, are taught every Saturday in conjunction with the Sabbath morning service in the synagogue. Interpretation and argument (*mussar* in yeshiva terminology— a word carrying ethical connotations) over these fundamental tenets of the Jewish religion come up through the study of the learned commentaries that constitute the Talmud.

Yossi Liphshitz, now in his late thirties, turned to secular studies after graduating from the Hebron Yeshiva, gained a matriculation certificate qualifying for university entrance, and now is an executive in Bikur Holim, one of Jerusalem's oldest hospitals. He remembers his life as a student with fondness and says his education there made secular studies later much easier. One receives the same impression from the work of Samuel Heilman, a professor of social anthropology in New York City's Queens College and a frequent visitor to Jerusalem's haredi community. He writes: "But having looked at the haredi community through the medium of my discipline, I shall never see it the same again. . . . This scene may bring tears of joy to Jews seeking to reanimate the vanished past. But in fact this is a museum exhibit replicating only a tiny segment of the Jewish world that was crushed by the Holocaust."

How accurate is this collective memory of the glorious past? Abraham Melamed, a member of the Israeli Knesset and a Holocaust survivor, claims that a century ago, when ten million Jews lived in Europe, most observed religious traditions—but only four thousand were full-time students in yeshivot. Some of those seminaries, notably Volozyin and Slobodka in Belorussia and Ponivezh in Lithuania, produced distinguished graduates. Chief Rabbi Abraham Isaac HaCohen Kook was a diligent scholar. Israel's national poet Haim Nachman Bialik escaped from his rigorous studies in Volozyin and started teaching Hebrew in the more liberal atmosphere of Odessa. Scholars still cite the many books on Jewish philosophy and learning written by graduates. But this tradition of creative scholarship did not survive the Holocaust. Professor Menachem Friedman of Bar-Ilan University, an authority on Israel's haredim, cites few if any breakthrough books written by graduates of Israeli yeshivot, who are deliberately isolated from daily life, which, in the nature of things, poses the most important questions confronting the contemporary meaning of ancient Jewish religion and culture. Even in the great Jewish centers of Eastern Europe where religion was closely interwoven with Jewish life, most young men worked for a living, and today in midtown Manhattan, Orthodox Jewish men in the full regalia of their sect are employed in the diamond trade, as salesmen in stores specializing in high-technology goods, and in law, accountancy, and finance. Many of them and all their children attend Jewish schools where, in addition to their religious studies, they must complete courses prescribed by the state for all students.

In Israel, the number of full-time yeshiva students in 2011 exceeded 120,000—a figure based on claims of the yeshivot themselves to calculate their subsidies. The Ministry of Education suspects the number is far less—below 100,000 students. Many are married with families and often inhabit the yeshiva compounds (*kolel*) to the age of forty-five and even beyond. This is the highest proportion of yeshiva students on record, anywhere at any time. Most of them are not gainfully employed (at least not officially) and are dependent on government and other financial support, or on the earnings of their wives who usually have to take jobs in addition to carrying the burden of care for their large families.

Why do they crowd into the yeshiva instead of following the ancient cherished Jewish tradition of Torah Va-Avodah— Hebrew for combining study with work? They ignore sayings such as those in the Babylonian Talmud: "Better to earn money by skinning an animal's carcass than by taking charity." There are a number of explanations for this Israeli phenomenon, but none have proven fully persuasive to the Israeli taxpayer, who foots the bill for this unique behavior.

On a practical level, joining a yeshiva seems the best and often is the only solution for eighteen-year-old boys whose earlier education has not included any core subjects that would have supplied them with the tools for earning a living in modern society except by physical labor. Furthermore, joining a yeshiva provides the haredi eighteen-year-old with an almost automatic exemption from the compulsory service of three years in the Israeli armed forces, although this excuse is not publicly advertised. In a community sense, the yeshiva study for males signifies commitment and loyalty, enhancing its prestige despite high economic sacrifice. Eli Berman, an economist at the University of California, San Diego, who specializes in the behavior of religious sects, studied the haredim and observed that as a result of the yeshiva's unique social environment many students, although exempt from army service by age, nevertheless decided to continue their yeshiva studies.

Moving to an almost mystical level, Israeli yeshiva studies provide an atmosphere that promotes a quest for a mysterious miracle known in Hebrew as *ness.* This concept defies one of the founding ideologies of the Jewish revival in Palestine, the "religion of labor," which exalted work that built settlements, drained swamps, and defended the homeland. This belief in salvation through physical labor contradicts the ideology of the Messianic haredim, who believe that by concentrating on their studies they will move closer to God. These are the conclusions of Dr. Nurit Stadler, a Hebrew University sociologist, in her study of Israeli haredim. She of course is aware that her conclusions defy traditional Jewish attitudes celebrating work, manual labor included. She views them as part of the haredi objections to Zionist ideals and the acquisitive nature of modern life, an element in the destruction of society, whether modern or traditional. But this mystical direction conflicts not only with Zionist ideals but above all with the teachings of the sages who tried to rebuild Jewish life on a new material basis after the destruction of the Second Temple in the year 70 CE.

The sages of the Mishna, the first book of laws written to adapt to a new life of a nation that had lost its political center, were deeply engaged in the workday world as they codified the tenets of Jewish life. They were practical, forward-looking Jewish moralists who two thousand years later are still known for their involvement in commerce and trade no less than their devotion to scholarship. Tradition honors personalities like Yochanan Hasandlar—John the Shoemaker—or Hillel Hazaken—the Old Hillel—who made his living as a chimney sweep but fixed his thoughts on how man should live in the world: "If I am not for myself, who shall be for me? But if I am only for myself, then what am I? And if not now, when?"

But today in Israel full-time yeshiva students make up a greater proportion of the population than in any other country.

According to a study by the OECD (Organization for Economic Cooperation and Development, a Paris-based government policy center for industrialized nations of which Israel recently became a member), 65 percent of all Israeli haredi men and 53 percent of haredi women between the ages of fifteen and sixty-five are unemployed, compared to 15 percent unemployed among non-haredi Israeli men. Among ultra-Orthodox Jewish males abroad, the percentage of nonworking males is much lower.

Extensive research by the Bank of Israel shows a marked increase in the participation of male haredim in Israel's labor force in recent years from 38 percent in 2009 to 45 percent in 2011. This expansion took place mainly in the business sector (from 18 percent in 2009 to 24 percent in 2011), and not just in religious education, which in the past employed the majority of the working ultra-Orthodox males. But even this rising percentage of gainfully employed haredim is very low compared to the more than 80 percent employment rate among Israeli males. The government has set a goal of 63 percent employment among haredi males by 2020, which seems highly unrealistic despite recent progress. Nevertheless, Professor Menachem Friedman of Bar-Ilan University is optimistic: he sees in the results of the study a changing mood within the haredi community and a desire to escape from the suffocating atmosphere in which the Torah, mainly in its literal interpretation, is the only accepted guide to life. The central bank study defines a haredi as someone whose last place of study was a yeshiva or who lives in an exclusively haredi settlement. But among haredi women, the rate of those gainfully employed is 60 percent. There also indications that a great many haredim are employed in undeclared jobs within their community, where they can avoid paying taxes.

This is supported by Esther Dominicini, former director of Israel's Social Security Institute, whose researchers had discovered prevailing tax evasion in the haredi community. Abraham Shochat, a popular minister of finance in several Labor-led governments, used to tell a not-so-humorous story, that when he suggested imposing an inheritance tax on very large estates he received anxious phone calls from several haredi Knesset members who argued that such a tax would be disastrous for many in their community. "How come?" wondered the minister. "I didn't know you people are rich. Don't they pay taxes?" The answer was no. "If they had paid taxes how could they afford to buy apartments for their children [studying] in the yeshiva?"

While yeshiva students receive a relatively small monthly living allowance of 855 shekels (about $225) from the government with no limit on the number of years they may study, no such scholarships are available for study in Israel's academic institutions, a cause of considerable resentment. Yet it creates a new reality, previously unknown in Jewish history, of Torah Bli Avoda —Torah without Work. At the same time the schools appear to be exaggerating their enrollment figures to obtain larger government block grants for themselves. An investigation by inspectors from the Education Ministry and the accountant general of the Finance Ministry concluded that the number of 120,000 yeshiva students claimed by the haredi schools was exaggerated by five to ten thousand. Their allocations for the year 2011 were reduced by 55 million shekels (about $15 million), and the police recommended criminal prosecution for fraud. That did not stop the Orthodox bloc in the Knesset from trying to extract additional concessions for yeshiva students on the calculation that the cost of maintaining a yeshiva student is lower than maintaining a student in an academic institution, especially in universities that finance Israel's celebrated research laboratories. Moshe Gafni, the outspoken haredi chairman of the Knesset's finance committee, has also begun advocating allowances for all students—but with qualifications defined in such a way by age, family status, and even car ownership so that almost the only beneficiaries would be those studying in yeshivot.

But core subjects are neglected in haredi schools, and they produce neither biblical nor scientific scholars. Surprisingly little attention is devoted to the Bible itself, the basic book of Jewish learning, which in Israel is of course taught in its original language, the mother tongue of every six-year-old child starting school. True, the first five books of the Bible are taught in connection with Sabbath services, and other books, including some of the prophets, are studied in the upper classes of some yeshivot. However, the wealth of biblical stories with their enriching imagery, the poetry and the psalms with their astoundingly rich language—all that is left mostly to the non-haredi schools. Every Independence Day, Israel holds a national Bible Contest, a popular televised event. But the contestants come mainly from secular and religious Zionist schools in Israel and abroad, not from the ultra-Orthodox schools. So, while the haredim are fundamentalists in the sense that they base their practice of Judaism on the words of the Bible, they actually concentrate on learning the rabbinical commentaries accumulated over past generations, not on the Bible itself. This arises from the ultra-Orthodox rabbis' fear that their followers will be exposed to what became known in the nineteenth century among Jewish and Gentile scholars as the Higher Criticism of the Bible. But to the ultra-Orthodox rabbis it is anathema to engage in this critical exercise of exchanging ideas about the deeper meaning of biblical texts lest it infect their own Bible studies and (more to the point) encourage independent thought that might undermine their own authority.

The obstacles imposed by the ultra-Orthodox establishment

have in fact not prevented an unprecedented expansion of secular education in various forms designed to help ultra-Orthodox youths trying to break out of the restrictive framework that condemns them to a life of poverty. One of the most optimistic actors in this massive effort is Professor Amiram Gonen of the Floersheimer Institute. Through the professor's contacts with donors, mainly in the United States and Canada, Gonen's group provides hundreds of scholarships each year to the Open University in Bat Yam, a coastal town near Tel Aviv; the Kiryat Ono College east of Tel Aviv; and other institutions. At the Open University, instruction is mainly by correspondence and does not require a high school certificate as an entrance requirement. (Similar adult education has been available with great success in Britain's Open University for more than thirty years.) Kiryat Ono College has initiated separate classes for ultra-Orthodox men and women offering law, accounting, English, and mathematics, as well as computer software and programming. In earlier years the number of women students, who do not go to yeshiva, was almost equal to the number of male students because the haredi men are burdened with large families while some of the women manage to stay in school. But more of the men are staying in school by at least one metric: the number of law students at Kiryat Ono has almost doubled from 136 in 2005 to 245 in 2011.

Meanwhile, the number of male students dropping out of the yeshivot was increasing sharply. In 2008, three researchers associated with the Jerusalem Institute of Studies, one of them formerly a student in a prominent yeshiva, surveyed five hundred men and women in the haredi school system and reported that 60 percent of them were interested in acquiring an academic education and 28 percent were willing to study outside the exclusively ultra-Orthodox framework. From conversations with haredim interested in running their own companies, it became clear that they realized that becoming directors required an academic degree, and therefore some were willing to leave the ultra-Orthodox cocoon.

But for these students, shifting from religious education presents unique problems. Even if the requirements of a high school certificate are waived, haredi students have to learn English, mathematics, and science as foundation courses before specializing in their chosen field. Most are older than secular students and must support a family while studying. The men are mostly between twenty-four and thirty, while 60 percent of the women who sign up for these secular studies are unmarried and supported by their parents. Haredi students themselves recognize that their dropout rate is higher than official figures—some say up to 20 percent. The men have to return to employment in physical labor to help support their families and cannot keep up with the demands of rigorous academic study. Many who take up pre-academic subjects also admit that they have to overcome psychological obstacles—not just opposition from family and friends but their own doubts and hesitations about loosening ties with their tightly knit community. Some admitted that during the first year they concealed their new courses of study from friends and family, often requiring complicated subterfuges. The Jerusalem Institute research paper recommended a number of organizational and educational aids, such as psychological and practical consulting units associated with the Ministry of Education and the Jerusalem Municipality, to help these students find their way toward a productive life.

Israel's academic institutions say they are ready to absorb former yeshiva students, but educating them at a higher level presents problems. Many are not sufficiently prepared, and they also insist on single-sex classrooms and, even worse, separation from their mainstream fellow students. This presents almost insuperable administrative problems for the universities and exerts continued downward pressure on the intake of haredi students. With the help of special government appropriations and foreign contributions to Professor Gonen and others, many academic preparatory courses offering core disciplines are now available. According to a survey of the Technion in Haifa, three thousand yeshiva students or former yeshiva students were enrolled in academic programs in 2011. While this number indicates phenomenal recent growth, it is still painfully small compared to the total number of yeshiva students. Most of these transfer students require not only a separate educational framework to prepare them for modern studies but often special conditions of employment as well.

Adina Bar-Shalom, the daughter of Rabbi Ovadia Yosef, the Shas leader, has established a college in Jerusalem for girls in pre-academic subjects. Similar colleges are in operation in B'nai Brak and also in the northern city of Safed, another center for the ultra-Orthodox. To the surprise of the Jerusalem Institute researchers, 71 percent of yeshiva students said they would be willing to add core studies to their morning religious classes. Today most yeshiva students do their pre-academic studies in the evenings in order not to force an immediate break with the haredi institutions that at best tolerate secular studies, which they label "extra-curricular activities." But this creates difficulties for those husbands who have pledged to assist their overburdened wives in caring for children in the large Orthodox families that have followed the biblical injunction to "be fruitful and multiply." In fact, the wives are also the breadwinners in most families, where it has long been considered an honor to support a learned husband steeped in study of Jewish law and tradition. And when the women work during the day, they expect their husbands to help in the evenings with the housework and child care.

While the drift of haredi students toward professional and academic education is no doubt encouraging, their numbers are still very small: in the hundreds or at most a few thousand. The main problem of ultra-Orthodox education will not be solved until the primary and secondary systems are drastically reformed. But to the ultra-Orthodox society and its leaders, these reforms are seen as a loss of control over their successor generation; they can be expected to resist bitterly. Whatever the disadvantages to the ultras of their decision to remain outside the workforce and subsist on state welfare, it remains a safeguard against their forced integration into a society with different priorities. As long as they have political leverage the haredim will use it. It will be up to the new generation of yeshiva students, who are more than ever aware of the world around them, to decide whether to remain compliant with the old order that separates them from the state in which they live or try to break out into the world of work, as well as serving the country that has sheltered and supported them while others have been willing to lay down their lives in its defense.

8

The Soldiers of Israel
or of God?

SIX THOUSAND MEN AND WOMEN, MOST OF THEM BELOW the age of thirty, 1 percent of the total Jewish population of Israel at that time, were killed in the war of 1948, when the state was established. About a similar number have fallen in wars and terror attacks since then. Yet the country is still besieged by the historic Arab and Persian enemies of the Jews and must depend on help from Jewry worldwide and its military alliance with the United States. Israel requires each young man and woman of eighteen to serve in the army for three years and then in the reserves. While the Druze and Circassians (Muslims of Russian descent who immigrated in the nineteenth century) as well as Bedouins serve the Israeli army, the six hundred thousand ultra-Orthodox Jews, who consider themselves more Jewish than all others, have been exempt from army service for sixty-four years and have threatened to revolt if their massive exemptions from the draft are not extended, or even if they are only amended.

The demand for a new conscription law arose from a ruling by Israel's Supreme Court ordering an end to the blanket exemption for yeshiva students by July 31, 2012. After the Netanyahu government's failure to negotiate a revision covering the haredim, the increasingly incendiary question was expected to land back in the Supreme Court with a request for an extension of several months to allow the army to devise a plan to defuse this political bombshell while somehow incorporating several thousand young haredim in its ranks.

Many other religious youths already fulfill their military obligations with enthusiasm. They are the inheritors of the traditions of the religious Zionist pioneers and today compose an important youthful cohort of the officer corps in some of the best fighting units. They can be identified by the knitted skullcaps that they wear. They seek "a more Jewish army" in contradiction to the hopes of David Ben-Gurion, who aspired for a "people's army" where all units would be equal with no separate ideology of its own. But what was originally a temporary exemption from army service granted to four hundred yeshiva students has become a national problem: more than half a million ultra-Orthodox youths do not serve in the army and also do not work, because taking a job would forfeit their exemption. Without some legislative intervention addressing the ultras' special status, about one-quarter of all Israeli men reaching the age of eighteen by 2020 are estimated to be automatically exempt from army service.

IT ALL BEGAN SEVERAL MONTHS BEFORE ISRAEL DECLARED ITS independence in 1948. Ben-Gurion ordered Israel Galili, chief of staff of what had until then been the Jewish Agency's underground army, the Haganah, to exempt students in religious seminaries. There were only about four hundred, and at the moment of peril for the new nation, there were few objections to having some rabbinical students pray for Israel's survival. The exemption was supported by the chief rabbi Yitzhak Halevi Herzog and carried a special significance in the shadow of the Nazi Holocaust, which destroyed much of Jewish culture in the course of murdering six million European Jews.

No one thought the exemption would be permanent. Nor were most Israelis aware of the fact that the number of students in the new yeshivot (for example, Ponivezh in B'nai Brak, named after the storied yeshiva by that name in Lithuania) would soon exceed that in the original yeshivot destroyed by the Nazis. Today, the percentage of full-time students in these religious seminaries in Israel represents the largest proportion of the total among Jewish communities anywhere at any time.

Politics soon played an even more important role in confirming and solidifying the military exemption, although it was never imagined that the numbers would become so large. Ben-Gurion had a strong interest in securing the support and indeed the adherence of the ultra-Orthodox community, many of whom actually withheld their formal allegiance from the new Jewish state until it would be governed by the Messiah. But whatever the political rationale for the exemption, it soon ran beyond all reason and control. No Israeli government has been able to end it. Secular left-wing parties have often adopted slogans condemning the exemption from service in the army. Posters proclaiming "One Army—One Draft" were raised in 1999 and helped to bring into power Ehud Barak, former chief of staff and Israel's most decorated soldier. By 2010, almost sixty thousand ultra-Orthodox men—about 10 percent of the total haredi population—were exempt not only from three years of compulsory military service but from the annual month of reserve duty demanded of all adults until after they reach the age of forty.

Politics have trumped military and civilian law: Galili's order was only temporary and did not bind the IDF when it was formed later out of the constituent fighting units, nor was it part of the status quo agreement of June 1947 between the Jewish Agency and Agudat Israel, the anti-Zionist haredi party. The IDF's religious obligations are limited to observance of the Sabbath, providing kosher food in all military installations, making religious services available to all soldiers who want to attend, and adhering to religious law in military burial.

Thus, while there was no legal basis for the yeshiva exemption, it became cemented into tradition if not law because the ultra-Orthodox insisted on it as a condition of support for governing coalitions. However, in 2002, the government, headed at that time by the Labor Party, was able to pass a law based on the report of a former Supreme Court justice, Tsvi Tal, himself an observant Jew, that attempted to find a way of convincing the haredim to join the army for one year in some national service, and then enter the labor market. Supporters argued that a large number of yeshiva students would choose army service as an opportunity leading to a civilian job. Employers often consider service history, rank, and technical courses when offering young veterans a job. Haredi politicians were equally aware that if doors to the secular world were opened for those who serve, they would be affected, too, but in the opposite way: they would lose influence over a cloistered, inward-looking group of young men. While this may seem short-sighted, there is no lack of evidence that the ultra-Orthodox leaders were determined to prevent these young and impressionable members of their flock from wandering to greener pastures.

The Knesset passed the law but with hesitation, and for a period of five years only. Its success with the Tal Law, as it is known by all, was very limited. Several hundred haredim, those who by their own admission did not see themselves fit to study in a yeshiva, volunteered each year to serve in special haredi battalions where only *glatt* kosher food was served and no women soldiers were to be found in their normal administrative jobs. Meanwhile, the majority of the haredi youths continued to pour into the crowded yeshivot upon reaching the age of eighteen. Even the few who volunteered for noncombatant public service insisted on doing so within the haredi community, thus increasing the burden on the government budget. When the first five years expired, the law was extended for another five years to 2012 for lack of a better solution.

While public opposition continued to rise against the ultra-Orthodox exemption and even Tal Law compromise, it became clear that another extension of the law without some kind of radical change would not be acceptable to the Israeli population as a whole. But at the same time, some began to doubt whether the haredim, or at least all of them, were needed in the Israeli army, which like most modern armies depends as much on technological skills to operate sophisticated modern weapons as it does on a sheer mass of men. Pilots and many other specialized military professionals require education as well as a commitment to serve many years so their skills are fully deployed. Few if any haredim fit those requirements. Moreover, until recently, Israel's demography, enhanced by one million immigrants from the Soviet Union and their children, provided the armed forces with enough eighteen-year-olds to fill the ranks of the infantry and other combat units, as well as the soldiers who served in units occupying the West Bank. Army manpower experts have also argued that the special requirements of the ultra-Orthodox soldiers, many of them married and with children who have to be supported, would constitute a special burden on the defense budget. These requirements included a rigorously kosher diet, three prayer periods a day, and the need to separate the ultra-Orthodox from other units.

Both the army and the haredim have reached a standoff. The number who joined up under the Tal Law provisions is negligible and has never risen above 4 percent of the haredim who reach the age of eighteen. Meanwhile, a civic group—composed mostly of parents of soldiers, high school students about to start their army service, lawyers, and housewives—has conducted a successful campaign demanding "equality in sharing the burden." After several demonstrations, the group appealed to Israel's Supreme Court arguing that the law was unconstitutional because it differentiates between two groups of citizens: those who have to serve in the army and those who not.

To the surprise of most Israelis the Supreme Court ruled in February 2012 that the Tal Law was indeed unconstitutional and could not be extended beyond its expiration in August of that year. The outgoing chief justice, Dorit Beinish, led the signers of the court's majority opinion on the ground that the law failed to follow the principles of equality and proportionality required by the Basic Law regulating the administration of justice—one of the few laws adopted by the Knesset that has assumed the status of constitutional law.

Beinish retired a week later at the mandatory age of seventy and was succeeded by Justice Asher Grunis, who had written the minority opinion in the appeal against the Tal Law. Grunis argued that the court had to be realistic, and that under present conditions the haredim could not be forced to serve like other young people of their age. From his minority opinion, the right-wing parties hoped that the new chief justice might lead a realignment of the court. They were quickly disappointed when, several days later, Grunis led a Supreme Court decision that rejected a compromise on a former ruling ordering the evacuation of a West Bank settlement for thirty families built at Ulpana Hill on privately owned Arab land near the larger religious settlement of Beit El near Jerusalem. Netanyahu's reaction was literally to buy out the illegal settlers by promising to build eight hundred new homes in other settlements—an overwhelming victory for the settler movement.

During Kadima's seventy-day partnership with the Netanyahu government, several compromise proposals were advanced extending special conditions to haredi recruits. A special parliamentary committee headed by Yochanan Plessner, a Kadima member of the Knesset, considered recruiting only twenty-three- or even twenty-five-year-old haredim (by which time most have children) or promising them special compensations for delaying yeshiva studies. At times it appeared that Netanyahu was prepared to confront and even override his haredi coalition partners, but in the end neither Netanyahu nor his defense minister Ehud Barak was able to produce a compromise that Kadima would accept—and the haredi leaders were unwilling to accept any compromise at all. The negotiations were further complicated by the insistence of Foreign Minister Avigdor Lieberman, leader of the party representing Russian immigrants, that not only the haredim but also all Arab Israelis must serve, if not in the army then at least in civilian positions, as teachers or police officers, for example—an idea vehemently opposed by Israeli Arab politicians and compromising their followers' allegiance to the Palestinian cause.

The simplest and probably most equitable solution would have the heads of the yeshivot select several hundred of their best and brightest graduates to advance to a higher level of study and avoid military service. But haredi politicians unanimously announced that they would reject such a solution. The fact is that the rabbis are more determined to keep their young students under their control than to allow them to be exposed even for a short time to a different environment where they might experiment with different styles of life. Chazon Ish, one of the spiritual leaders of Agudat Israel, gave the game away in one of the leaflets widely circulated to defend the haredi position: "However much I fear the restrictions that the state will impose on our young generation, what I fear more is that they would like them."

When the Tal Law expired at the start of August 2012 without any legislative successor, all yeshiva students were theoretically subject to the draft. Like other Israeli Jews, they should receive a notice to report for duty on their eighteenth birthday, prompting Defense Minister Barak to declare with satisfaction in a radio interview: "All Israelis are now in an equal position." He hardly could have meant it, because he made it clear that the army authorities will decide who will be called to serve "in accordance with their mobilization needs." This puts the army in a dilemma that will take many months, and probably an election, to play out. If the generals dare to draft the haredim, the rabbis can summon their followers to demonstrate in the streets—and these young men have a propensity to riot. But if the military follows the lead of the politicians and ducks the issue by simply passing over the names of thousands of yeshiva boys, the dispute cannot hang in limbo for long. Lawsuits against the minister of defense will be justified on the ground of equal treatment under the law. The irony of Ehud Barak, Israel's most decorated soldier, being sued for exempting citizens from defending the homeland would be lost on no one, least of all Barak himself and certainly not on the judges of Israel's Supreme Court. They will be confronted with clear evidence that the army is not drafting all eligible youngsters. Sooner or later the government and the Knesset will have to deal with the subject that Netanyahu and Barak preferred to push aside: can an equal draft be ignored in a democracy?

For those seeking an end to the special exemption for the haredim, the dispute reaches even beyond questions of justice under the law or equality and proportionality. The debate affects the existence of the nation as a homeland for Jews. Military service is the principal activity unifying a society composed of many immigrant groups. Literature, music, art, and especially the humor of everyday life are influenced by the nation's universal military experience and help establish long-term friendships as well life-long career networks. The IDF was not intended to be a melting pot, but it fulfills that essential role in Israeli society.

By deliberately avoiding this rite of passage, yeshiva students carry a mark on their records even if they try to integrate into Israeli society, as many of them do. As a result, for the past sixty years two different kinds of Jews have been evolving, who hardly know each other as individuals and understand their divergent values even less. Their links are ever more tenuous and their relations more distant and adversarial. Even in areas of disagreement such as Sabbath observance and the values of Judaism that offer some common ground, the ability for the two sides to explore it together may have been lost.

9

Steel Helmets and
Knitted Skullcaps

A LONELY CLOTH BANNER SHOCKED THE ISRAELI PUBLIC
when it was unveiled in 2009 at Judaism's holiest site:
THE GOLANI BRIGADE DOES NOT EVICT SETTLERS FROM
THEIR HOMES. The young recruits, sworn in at Jerusalem's Western Wall at a traditionally solemn national ceremony of solidarity and affirmation, were protesting the role that the Israeli army
could be ordered to play in taking down unauthorized settlements that have been hastily erected by right-wing zealots in the
occupied West Bank. Protests are common in Jerusalem, but
the real shock of this particular incident was the realization that
the army could face a revolt against civilian authority, especially
since the then-recently formed Israeli government of Prime
Minister Netanyahu and his defense minister Ehud Barak
appeared weak and unfocused in dealing with the peace process.
The ruling majority was making only feeble attempts to meet
what was then the Obama administration's urgent demand to
stop the unauthorized settlements.

The incident was brief. The banner was removed and the

recruits were severely punished; the army withdrew its annual financial subsidy of 800,000 shekels (about $200,000) to the Hesder Yeshiva Har Grizim, a military-religious yeshiva on the West Bank where the recruits had studied. But a warning light was lit: can all units of the Israeli army be trusted to obey orders if one day an Israeli government signs a peace agreement with the Palestinian authority to withdraw from the West Bank or even part of it?

FROM THE FOUNDING OF THE STATE, BEN-GURION HIMSELF feared the disaster of an ideological split in the military when he molded rival militias into the IDF and was ready to battle, literally, against both right and left on the issues of internal cohesion and political neutrality. When the rightist Irgun attempted to smuggle arms into the new state in 1948 aboard the *Altalena*, Ben-Gurion did not hesitate to order shore batteries to sink her off a Tel Aviv beach. The following year he fought and defeated some of his closest Labor associates in forcing the dissolution of the Palmach, then the backbone of the army, and its absorption into the IDF. Ben-Gurion adamanatly pursued this policy by refusing to invite representatives of the Mapam Party to join his government because of their plan to politicize the nascent army by creating some leftist military units in the unified military force.

But sixty years later, when Ben-Gurion's vision of army-above-party had long prevailed, the danger of politicizing the armed forces was reawakened, above all by the undisciplined settler youth. But they did not act unbidden by some of their rabbis and teachers—as well as the example of soldiers on active service who refused to obey orders blocking the settlers from "taking over areas in the Land of Israel"—Eretz Israel, once a biblical prophecy but now a political slogan charged with religious meaning. In 2009, after the government's decision to suspend construction for ten months in the West Bank, the issue reemerged with new force. Should a soldier obey his officer conveying his government's commands or his rabbi bearing the commands of God?

The dilemma developed into a political crisis following belligerent statements by Rabbi Eliezer Melamed, the head of the Har Bracha yeshiva, near Nablus, where the Golani recruits had trained. Melamed told his students they were expected to obey the orders of their rabbis rather than those of their officers. The rabbi also declined an invitation to meet with Defense Minister Barak, after which his yeshiva lost its government grant. This decision caused a storm, and some rabbis even suggested that their students refuse to serve in the army on the ground that "Torah is our belief." Most of the rabbis of similar yeshivot adopted a more moderate stance and even obliged Rabbi Melamed to issue a conciliatory statement. But the dispute festered. A former IDF chief of staff, Amnon Lipkin-Shahak, remarked: "The rabbis may have climbed down from their high tree, but they left in place a ladder so that they could climb up again at any time they choose."

Things have not always been this way. The religious Zionist movement, and especially its pioneering wing, was a solid partner of Ben-Gurion's Labor Party in the 1930s, when its members established the first kibbutzim in the upper Jordan Valley, Tirat Tzvi and Sede Eliahu, as well as Yavneh and Sa'ad in the southern coastal plain. Thus, in the 1950s the left wing of the religious Zionists and most of their Knesset members were loyal supporters of the early governments led by Ben-Gurion's Mapai. During the 1948 war, hundreds of the religious Zionist pioneers were killed defending the settlements of Gush Etzion in the Judean hills, fighting alongside the secular Haganah soldiers against the well-organized troops of Jordan's British-led Arab Legion.

But in the 1960s, the first signs of a political switch by the religious Zionists began when a group led by Zevulun Hammer and Yehuda Ben Meir, who became advocates of Greater Israel, clearly moved to the right on religious as well as political issues. The victories and territorial conquests of the Six-Day War in 1967 intensified the transformation of the religious right, so that by the end of the century it had almost entirely disappeared as supporters deserted to more radical splinter parties.

After the Six-Day War the younger leaders of the religious Zionists established Gush Emunim (the Bloc of the Faithful) to coordinate, finance, and plead the case of the settler movement. First hundreds and later thousands of their sympathizers established settlements in the West Bank, the Gaza Strip, and even areas of the Sinai desert that clearly were destined to be returned to Egypt. Not all the settlers were animated by religious belief or even motivated politically. Many (some believe even the majority) aspired for a better life outside the constraining borders of pre-1967 Israel. Budgets for building houses and military protection were amply provided by the Israeli government. Administrative jobs in education, security, and small industries were available. Some settlements became mainly bedroom communities offering commuters larger and more modern houses. On the level of political ideology the gap between the religious Zionists and the haredim had widened since the Six-Day War when it looked to the Zionists as though the Messiah could be brought by hard work and military aggressiveness and not merely by prayer and religious studies. But on the level of religious devotion, the two camps appeared to be getting closer by the day, because religion helped justify the settlers' expansionist cause.

In the first years after moving to the West Bank, the settlers faced opposition from a secular establishment that objected to

Gush Emunim's attempt to achieve the right wing's political goal of Eretz Israel Hashlema—an undivided Land of Israel in its historic biblical boundaries. The leaders of the movement, Rabbi Moshe Levinger, Hanan Porat, and others, had a charismatic, even magical influence that extended to their political opponents including Shimon Peres, then minister of defense and later president, and the poet Haim Guri. These onlookers were mesmerized by the settlers' messianic zeal and continued to support them in spirit and in private while opposing them in public. These "facts on the ground" created a political reality that inevitably led to a clash not only with the Palestinians but also with Israel's friends abroad, including the government of the United States, to say nothing of the rhetorical ammunition these expansionist aims gave to Israel's detractors in Europe.

For the religious Zionist youth the spectacular victory in June 1967 was not just a historic military accomplishment but also a blessing by God. If the Almighty had stretched out his arm to help Jewish fighters in their most perilous moment, who were the secularist politicians to yield the fruits of victory and withdraw to former demarcation lines that, as everybody agreed, were temporary and had no geographic or strategic logic? This controversial reasoning appealed to a large segment of the Israeli public, including some with a secular, progressive upbringing. But the dilemma of the religious Zionists' dual loyalties was exposed by the withdrawal from Israel's official settlements in Gaza ordered by Ariel Sharon's government in 2005. This was Israel's first withdrawal, designed as a peaceful gesture from a place teeming with hostility that Israel had never sought to conquer from the Arabs. "Let them choke on it," Defense Minister Moshe Dayan said during the 1967 deliberations of the war council that decided to bypass Gaza altogether.

Fortunately, there were only minor breaches of discipline as the army finally pulled out of Gaza almost forty years later, yet one consequence was the appearance of a group calling itself Hilltop Youth. These youngsters came mainly from the hesder yeshivot established by the religious Zionists to combine Talmudic study with military service. They adopted methods of violent resistance against both the police and the army, ostensibly without the support of their own movement, and took their name from their tactic of moving swiftly from one West Bank hilltop to another to defend their illegal but strategically situated settlements overlooking Arab land. In some cases the Hilltop Youth gangs claimed to be taking revenge on the Israeli authorities by destroying neighboring Palestinian property.

This transition of the religious Zionists from a moderate to an extreme political movement—separatist, nationalist, and messianic in its own way—is no isolated phenomenon. Although the ideological gap between the religious Zionists and the haredim has remained and even widened in many respects, the two camps have moved much closer on religious ideology and practice. Half a century ago, boys and girls studied and played together in religious Zionist schools and in their youth movement B'nai Akiva. Today they are mostly separated. The boys have adopted the fashion of wearing their shirts outside their trousers so the fringes on the four corners of their mini prayer shawls are clearly visible as a sign of both their faith and politics, while the girls hide their hair under kerchiefs.

In their religious practices today there is hardly a difference between these extremist Zionist settlers and the ultra-Orthodox haredim, although in their goals, or rather in the methods by which they hope to achieve them, they are generations apart. While these Zionists believe that aggressive action will enable them to control the Land of Israel from the sea to the Jordan River, the haredim believe that mere prayer and study will bring the Messiah, and with him full title to the Land of Israel. It is no wonder, therefore, that even serious and well-informed writers such as David Remnick confuse the odious acts of the two groups. In a commentary in *The New Yorker* magazine on March 12, 2012, Remnick condemned the ultra-Orthodox for spitting at a nine-year-old girl on her way to school for supposedly not being "properly dressed," but also for the despicable warning of Rabbi Elyakim Levanon of a hesder yeshiva that soldiers should prefer "a firing squad" to being forced to listen to women singing. Anybody familiar with Israeli conditions knows that the very few ultra-Orthodox soldiers actually serving in the IDF would never be ordered to listen to the songs of women soldiers. Characters like Levanon are just a noisy minority among the religious Zionist rabbis. Rabbi Eli Sadan, founder of the first hesder yeshiva, was furious at Levanon for employing such "halachic terminology" against the army. Sadan published his criticism of Levanon in *Orot*, a publication of the movement, which was then picked up by the Internet publication *Ynet* and received a large number of approving comments.

What explains this metamorphosis among the religious Zionist youth? In a 1996 article entitled "Religious Zionism—From Radical Zionism to Religious Fanaticism," the political scientist Avner Horowitz of Ben-Gurion University in Beersheba traced it back to the messianic ideology of the revered chief rabbi Abraham Isaac HaCohen Kook, and especially that of his son Zvi Yehuda Kook. According to Horowitz, Rabbi Kook the father was aware of the nineteenth-century gap between the Enlightenment's intellectual awakening among Jews and the simultaneous atrophy of Jewish intellectual discourse, and was determined to reanimate Jewish spiritual thought and bridge the divide. In his vision, the Jews' return to Zion and their establishment of agricultural settlements were part of the coming of the Messiah. To elaborate on this, he turned to neo-Hegelian dialectics: the seeds of the future were already evident in the secular rejection of religion, which he viewed as an inevitable stage in the path of religious redemption, which emerged in the pioneering element of religious Zionism and lasted until 1967. From 1967 onward, the impetus came from the Merkaz Ha-rav (Center of the Rabbi) yeshiva in Jerusalem run by Rabbi Zvi Yehuda Kook. There his disciples found a spiritual cause in their military service, which characterized the center of the movement as opposed to such fringes as the Hilltop Youth. Rabbi Kook preached the slogan of "the Book and the Sword," and his pupils, their heads covered by *kippa sruga*—knitted skullcaps—eagerly volunteered to serve in the army. More and more devoted young men with knitted skullcaps are joining the officer corps of the infantry, armored corps, and paratroopers, and even such special elite units as the naval commandos and the air force. In many of these units they must volunteer to serve for a number of years or even make the army their career, so their role in the military is not just a passing fashion. And though most of these religious volunteers hold to their Orthodox upbringing, some are swayed by the more permissive life of their secular comrades, thus increasing the fear of the haredi leadership of losing control over the next generation if they are conscripted like all other Israeli Jews.

While Ben-Gurion insisted that all army units should be equal and shed any political and sectional taint, he allowed one exception: the establishment of the Nachal units. Nachal, short for Noar Chalutzi Lochem (Fighting Youth), represented a concession to the political left to compensate for the weakening of pioneer youth movements after the establishment of the state. These groups had grown out of the kibbutz movement and gave some satisfaction to the veterans of the Palmach after their own units were broken up and integrated into the new IDF. Nachal units were allotted time for work on the land and organizational efforts to build new settlements for the expanding population. During the first decades of the state this special corps seemed to be fulfilling its dual mission; Nachal units excelled in battle even though they had less military training. But as the weapons of the IDF, like those of all modern armies, became more technologically sophisticated, Nachal's highly motivated recruits no longer were necessarily the best, and the prestige of their units gradually dwindled within the military.

Yet the fact that the IDF had allowed special units with their own training schedules and goals beyond a strictly military mission provided a convenient precedent for the religious Zionist movement to demand its own separate units. They emerged mostly after the victories of the Six-Day War led to the establishment of dozens of hesder yeshivot. They are in effect in part-time seminaries where the soldiers do religious study for several months during their three years of army service (*hesder* means "by special arrangement"). The establishment of settlements in the occupied territories of the West Bank of Jordan attracted many of the graduates of the hesder yeshivot, which in turn led to heated conflicts with the army commanders like the incident of the banner at the Western Wall.

Another source of controversy in the IDF was the role of the army's chief chaplain and his position in the army's hierarchy. For many years after the founding of the state, the chief education officer was generally considered the dominant source of cultural and even spiritual guidance for soldiers. He approved not only the list of speakers and cultural events in army camps but also seminars and educational tours to historic places. Several of those who accepted the coveted post were established writers and educators who viewed their main responsibility as raising the young soldiers' morale and broadening their historical outlook. The role of the chief chaplain in those years was mainly religious—arranging prayer services, assisting and presiding at weddings and funerals, and ensuring that food was prepared and served according to dietary laws. The task of providing spiritual support to soldiers in distress was soon taken over by mental health officers.

Some military rabbis of the early days achieved special recognition for the way they accomplished their mission. Most prominent among them was no doubt Rabbi Shlomo Goren who appeared at the Western Wall in Jerusalem, blowing the shofar, the traditional ram's horn, and holding a heavy Torah scroll soon after it was captured in the Six-Day War in 1967. Goren also tried to identify the spot where Moses was handed the tablet of the Ten Commandments on Mount Sinai close to the present Santa Catherina Greek Orthodox Monastery, and he devoted much energy and the influence of his office to the formal conversion to Judaism of many soldiers whose religious identity was in dispute. From time to time, army chaplains have tried to expand their role and replace the chief education officer by introducing more lectures and tours in an attempt to persuade soldiers to become more observant Jews.

The Israeli state controller, Micha Lindenstrauss, turned to the growing influence of the army chaplains in his annual report issued in 2012. He described at great length how rabbis who insist that they are fighting for "the Jewish consciousness" have gained the upper hand in confrontations with individual officers and even some of the high command. The chaplains conduct tours for soldiers to places with controversial political significance; for example, they get help, from the Elad group, which campaigns to spread the writ of Judaism in Jerusalem's Old City by settling in its Arab houses. The report names officers and officials of the Defense Ministry who support the chaplains, starting with no less than the ministry's director general, Udi Shani. The controller also singled out Colonel Avidgor Ronsky as one of the most influential army chaplains in recent years. A brilliant soldier who was "born again" to Orthodox Judaism, Ronsky targeted less effective army education officers by accusing them of being homosexuals. In articles in the army magazine *Bamachaneh* he called other officers "defeatist." After his term as chief chaplain ended, Ronsky decamped to an extremist West Bank settlement to continue his campaign.

Army service by women has also become a focus of acute controversy because of Orthodox pressure. Women fighters were an absolute necessity in the War of Independence, when any hand that could hold a gun or drive a vehicle was desperately needed. The tradition began in the Haganah and the other Jewish underground armies and was continued when women served in the British army during World War II; more than twenty-five hundred Jewish women from Palestine served in various British units mostly in the Middle East. Yet when the War of Independence ended in 1949, objections arose from various political groups. The government yielded, and although it continued to conscript all Jewish eighteen-year-olds of both sexes, women were permitted to serve two years instead of three and would be exempt if they declared that they conducted "a religious way of life" that was inimical to military life. The law specifically indicates that women who claim this religious exemption must "maintain Kashrut and observe the Sabbath." These domestic conditions are in fact not strictly monitored by the army authorities, and few women have been investigated and even fewer prosecuted for violating the conditions of being excused from active service. This does not prevent the majority of most secular girls of eighteen from entering the military and fulfilling an essential role in the administrative and technical services, in intelligence, and even in instructing the men in the use of weapons, including heavy vehicles such as armored personnel carriers. Women are seldom included in combat units, but in 2011 a woman officer, Major General Orna Barivai, became the first female commander of the IDF personnel.

In 2011, women in uniform also became the topic of another controversy centered on the question of whose orders a young soldier should obey—that of his officer or his rabbi? The question focused on military women's choirs. Should religious soldiers be allowed to walk out of an army performance by women singers? This proved to be a perhaps marginal but nonetheless emotional provocation among religious young men. Some rabbis ordered their followers to avoid any musical event in which women participated. And from that arose the slinging match between the two rabbis over whether listening to their female comrades sing represented a fate worse than death by a firing squad.

The source of the Talmudic ordinance prohibiting the public singing of women (vulgarly expressed by comparing a woman's voice to her sexual organ) is in itself controversial. There are several descriptions in the Bible of women like Moses's sister Miriam singing and dancing in front of men. Some scholars argue that the prohibition originated when the authors of the Talmud were disturbed by the singing of gentile women on their household staff. In any case, the prohibition is not widely observed. Orthodox men can be seen in every concert in which mixed choirs of men and women sing classical and popular music. Female singers performed in concerts sponsored by the Jerusalem Municipal Council, which includes representatives of Orthodox parties in the governing coalition.

Yet in 2011 when a mixed army choir performed on the festive occasion of the coveted officers' school of the Israeli Army, four cadets ignored a warning from their superiors and walked out; they were dropped from the course leading to a commission. The incident touched off a public debate that ended only when the chief of staff, Lieutenant General Benny Ganz, confirmed the continuing participation of women singers at festive military occasions. Yet the voices of those who object to women singing in public will most likely be heard again—not from the religious Zionist militants but from the haredim, who isolate themselves from the wider world while trying to impose their values on it.

1 0

Discrimination
Against Women

ALL THE WORLD KNOWS THAT WOMEN SERVE ALONGSIDE
men in Israel's citizen army. Equality may not be total,
especially in combat units, but women perform essential
military tasks from driving heavy vehicles, including trucks and
tank transporters, to serving in top secret intelligence units. This
departure from Jewish tradition, which still separates men and
women in many synagogues, was an essential part of the secular
and communitarian tradition of Jewish Palestine. It was recognized three years after the founding of the State of Israel when the
Knesset adopted a law in 1951 aimed at eliminating centuries of
discrimination against women in Judaism. Eliminating it on paper,
anyway.

Although the Bible features heroines like Moses's sister
Miriam, the prophet Deborah, and Yael, the heroine who killed
the tyrant Sisra, Jewish tradition had for many generations dis-
credited women. For more than two thousand years in the Diaspora, few women were taught to read and write, and they were

usually daughters of learned men, like Rashi's daughters in the tenth century. Because they were illiterate, women were excluded from most official functions; they attended religious services as observers, from their special balcony in many synagogues, rather than reading from sacred texts as participants. After Jews began migrating to Jerusalem in the mid-nineteenth century to escape emancipation, no schools were provided for women. Only after the first schools were established there by Jewish organizations abroad did some include classes for girls.

The law entitled Equal Rights for Women proclaimed "principles to ensure full equality between men and women in the spirit of the principles of the Declaration of Independence of the State of Israel," but the devil is always in the details, and the truth emerged a few paragraphs below: the marital condition of women, which profoundly affects their legal status, depends on rulings by the rabbinical and not the civil courts. Paragraph five, the law that supposedly gives equal rights to women, in fact gives them right back to the rabbis: "Marriage and Divorce: this law does not intend to impinge upon prohibitions and permissions concerning marriage and divorce." A Jewish woman planning to marry must follow the demeaning "instructions" of a marriage adviser—a woman employed by male rabbis. Whatever her individual beliefs, she is obliged by religious ritual to take a bath called a *mikvah*.

Once married, if a woman seeks a divorce, even from a physically abusive husband, Israel's equal-rights law offers her no defense. She must throw herself on the mercy of the rabbinical court, on which no woman can sit. Specially qualified women pleaders are permitted to defend female clients before the court—a privilege finally granted by the rabbinical judges only in this century. And divorce itself is not clear-cut. Although a woman can ask a civil court to adjudicate her claims on marital property and her demand for alimony and child support, no Orthodox rabbi will officiate at her second marriage if her husband refuses to agree to a divorce. This puts her in a special category known as *mesorevet get*, which literally means she has been refused a divorce. The rabbinical courts also have the right to compel a widow to marry her husband's brother. If she refuses, she must undergo a humiliating ceremony called *halitza*; the Torah prescribes that a shoe be thrown at her at the gate of the city. The ceremony is rarely performed.

A very small number of teachers of Jewish law have recently ruled that women can serve as judges in rabbinical courts. But nevertheless they continue to be banned from the rabbinical bench. Never mind that the Bible's Book of Judges says of the prophet Deborah: "The people of Israel went up to her for judgment." Even the great Jewish sage Maimonides brushed aside the Bible with his own gloss: Deborah, he argued in the twelfth century, was only an adviser to the judges of Israel. And he argued further that her only authority as a judge derived from the defendants' agreement to permit her to judge them.

A surprisingly large number of cases in which women have been victims of an obvious miscarriage of justice are brought before the rabbinical courts. In one widely reported case in 2011, a wife who took refuge with her daughter in a Jerusalem hostel for battered women was refused a divorce, even though a civil court found her husband guilty of assault and sentenced him to eight months of prison, denying his three appeals. The rabbinical judge, Israel Yfrach, ordered a forced reconciliation between the two when her husband got out of jail. Needless to say, the battered wife still demanded a divorce. As for the judge, he was promoted to head the rabbinical court in Jerusalem. The chief Sephardic rabbi, Shlomo Amar, promoted him despite admitting that Judge

Yfrach's service had been problematical, but he claimed he had no other candidate.

Religious law also prohibits the marriage of a divorcée to certain religious officials; the ban is part of civil law precisely because rules of marriage and divorce have been ceded to the religious courts. Traditionally, Jews are divided into three groups, the Kohanim, or priests in the Temple; the Levites, who serve as the priests' assistants; and the common people, or the Israelites. The rabbinical ruling is based on Leviticus 21:7, which specifies that a Kohen may not marry "a prostitute or harlot nor a divorcee." The basis for the ban in Jewish law is the necessity to preserve priestly purity—never mind that Jews have not had priests to officiate at religious rites since the Romans destroyed the Second Temple in Jerusalem during the Jewish revolt in the first century. (Today's rabbis—the word means teacher or master—cannot officiate at a public service of worship without at least nine other Jewish men being present in what is called a minyan.) After two thousand years, the Kohanim are highly unlikely to accept the loss of status implied by the right to officiate. Perhaps they might regain their priestly office in the equally unlikely event that a Third Temple is built. Even if many named Cohen, Kagan, Katz, Azulai, and others denoting priestly descent were willing to forfeit a virtually mythical right to serve in the Temple, Israel's rabbinate are too stubborn to change their ancient rules.

Women suffer discrimination in other ways. A woman does not automatically inherit assets from a father who has sons. The sons are anointed heirs by Jewish law and are in turn charged with providing for the needs of their mother and sisters from the inheritance. These needs are defined by the sons, and they do not necessarily include providing them an education. Jewish law says that the marital tie is based on the fact (actually a supposition) that a man symbolically buys his wife with her knowledge and free consent. Men are only asked to honor their wives, but wives are bound to obey husbands, who can disregard their marital vows.

Debate over these ancient rules—as honored in the breach by modern Israelis as in their observance—is as old as the early Jewish settlements in Palestine. In 1953 Moshe Sharett, then acting prime minister, introduced a bill to regulate rabbinical courts. He argued to the Knesset that Jewish law "requires very many people to compromise on basic principles of modern life." He accused the rabbis of making "a shameful claim, which no one really takes seriously," that Jews had already made great progress toward equality in the last thousand years. That was an allusion to Rabbenu Gershom, who lived and taught in France back in the tenth century. That medieval rabbi, known as Light of the Exile, in effect stopped Jewish men from taking more than one wife, from having concubines, and from divorcing their wives without their consent. Despite these prohibitions—radical for their day— women were still not permitted to be their fathers' inheritors; they depended on men to guarantee and in effect to control their fate.

These rulings were accepted by most contemporary Jewish communities in France and Germany, although not in distant and isolated Yemen. They were meant to be temporary, probably to bring Jews in line with the Christian communities where they had settled, but to this day they prevail. But, as Sharett pointed out, the modern-day rabbis used Gershom's millennium-old domestic reforms to support the ludicrous argument that Jewish law had not become fossilized. Gershom's ruling must be understood against the background of the Christian society surrounding the Jews. From Carolingian times, polygamy had been banned in

Christian society. The rise in the economic status of the Jews and their concern for the status of their daughters induced them to give religious approval to the custom of monogamy that in fact was already in force in the Jewish community at the time.

In later centuries the position of Jewish women in the Diaspora improved, mainly as the result of the influence of their non-Jewish surroundings. But outside influence proved retrograde under Ottoman rule. Each of the thirteen ethnic-religious communities in Palestine had internal autonomy in local civil and religious matters, which included the status of women. In the haredi community they had no vote and limited rights of inheritance, and were forbidden even to study the Torah or read it in public. By contrast, secular groups could opt to follow the civil laws that prevailed in the general society. Under the British mandate, which followed the collapse of the Ottoman Empire at the end of World War I, the situation was almost reversed. The British established the Vaad Leumi—the National Council—as an umbrella group to represent the Jewish community before the mandate authorities; it was composed of both the secular political parties and religious Zionists. The ultras opted out and stood on their own.

Even the religious Zionists in Palestine realized that they were part of a basically secular movement and gave women the right to vote in the early twentieth century, just as they were achieving it in Britain and elsewhere. But this only deepened the rift with the haredim, and political considerations then forced the religious nationalists to reconsider. Chief Rabbi Kook, an ally of the religious Zionists under the British mandate, had always been a leader in opposing women's voting rights, but not all religious groups agreed. Then, when Israel's founding assembly decided to grant the women the vote, the ultra-Orthodox parties gave their passive consent, if only to gain a larger representation in the Knesset. Ben-Gurion and his ruling labor majority knew very well that the ultra-Orthodox would insist on the principle that "the honor of a woman is in her home" but only up to the point when the price of maintaining the principle became too high.

Not surprisingly, the haredim have never put a woman's name on the party lists from which Knesset representatives are selected, although the religious Zionist parties have allowed women to serve. In the last months of 2011 Israeli public opinion was insulted when the faces of women were deliberately distorted in group pictures in haredi dailies. Advertisements showing women were systematically torn off public bulletin boards in Israel. Clothing advertisers have to exercise self-censorship, while haredi leaders have learned not to carry their campaign too far. But wives of great Hasidic rabbis are often shown special favoritism; their pictures are allowed to appear in haredi publications.

The haredi press repeatedly downplays stories of divorce especially between ultra-Orthodox couples. The argument in favor of such censorship is that such items reflect on the honor of the Jewish family, where long-term bonds are valued. A similar attitude blankets articles about homosexuality and lesbianism, which are considered sinful in Jewish tradition. Roy Lachmanovitz, a former press officer of the Shas ultra-Orthodox party, has called on the haredi press to ignore all such stories lest they encourage imitation among the faithful.

The contradictions between the traditional Jewish law and the broad principles in the Declaration of Independence became painfully clear as soon as the new state took over the mixed inheritance of Ottoman and British civil and criminal law. Civil law defined citizenship, as it does in any democratic country. But the law also retained the Ottoman concept of religious communities, even down to their designation on Israel's national identity cards—which made a mockery of the Declaration's promise of equal rights "without distinction of religion, race or sex" as well as "freedom of conscience, education and culture." For women, these promises were badly smudged if not wiped away entirely by making all Israeli Jews subject to rabbinical instead of civil law in marriage and divorce. (Arab citizens of Israel live under their own family law.)

Male judges are often reluctant to order a divorce—known as a *gett*—when the husband refuses to agree and to pay alimony. In most cases the courts do not even dictate when the divorce papers have to be delivered and when alimony payments must start. Often no final date is imposed for the divorce to become effective. Husbands thus can easily evade the rabbinical courts or even simply disappear, since the judges cannot invoke police power. In theory they have the right to impose sanctions on rebellious husbands, including denying the extension of driving licenses or even blocking bank accounts, but are reluctant to do so on the argument that they would be "fabricating divorces" even if husband and wife agree. The worst consequence of the appointment and promotion of misogynist judges is the often insuperable barriers to divorce. In an attempt to overcome the general distaste for the rabbinical courts, in 2012 the Sephardic chief rabbi Shlomo Amar supported several religious members of the Knesset in pushing through a measure obligating the rabbinical judges to punish husbands who disobey their orders or be subject to punishment themselves.

Shulamit Aloni, formerly a Knesset member and a minister in several governments, has emerged as Israel's political leader in the demand for women's rights. A lawyer and journalist, her credentials as a patriot date from her frontline service in the city of Jerusalem during the 1948 war, when she was captured by Jordanian forces. Her argument is grounded in the Declaration of Independence, which does not even hint at the existence of religious communities that make women subservient in their private lives. Ms. Aloni, taking the role of America's nineteenth-century abolitionists, argues that the State of Israel, itself the product of modern ideas, has not completed the task of consolidating itself as a secular state.

Prejudices against secular women have accumulated in the rabbinical courts. The rabbinical judges commonly force children to transfer out of secular to religious schools at the demand of a divorced father. Such rulings merely intensify the bitterness of the divorced wife and prompt her to seek ways of evading the law. All matters of personal status that affect both men and women are decided in the rabbinical courts—which are in effect family courts—but there are no women judges. Only in recent years were women allowed to be represented by lawyers of their own sex. Almost twenty years ago, a courageous woman from Yerucham, a town in the Negev populated mainly by North African Jews, succeeded in breaking the taboo preventing women from participating in the local religious councils that oversee synagogues, ritual baths, and the preparation of kosher food. A survey in April of that year disclosed that only twenty-two women were chosen among the 450 members of the councils appointed by Ya'akov Margi, a member of the ultra-Orthodox Shas Party serving as minister of religion in the Netanyahu government. Rabbi Ovadia Yosef, the spiritual leader of Shas, rebuked this minister from his own party for not appointing more women.

It is possible for a couple to avoid the harsh restrictions of rabbinical marriages by living together without a religious ceremony; the woman is recognized as "being known in public" (*yedu'ah ba'tzibur*) as the man's life partner. Even after her partner's death, the civil courts preserve her rights as a tenant, protect her inheritance, and transfer pension rights even without the existence of a clear-cut contract or a formal will. This precedent arose after several claims were lodged by women whose partners had been killed fighting in Israel's wars.

A simpler way to escape the severity of the Orthodox rabbinical restrictions is to marry abroad in a civil ceremony. From the first days of statehood, the Interior Ministry has been legally obliged to register a Jewish couple from abroad who present the traditional Jewish marriage contract known as a *ketuba*—but only when signed by an Orthodox rabbi. But the law also directs the ministry to accept a civil marriage license, and this dual track can lead to almost comical contradictions. In one case, the bride, an American citizen, was married in New York to a native Israeli, in a religious ceremony performed by her father, a Conservative rabbi. When the couple settled in Israel, the groom presented himself at the Ministry of the Interior to update his status from "bachelor" to "married" on his Israeli identity card. The Israeli officials refused to recognize the marriage contract because it was signed by a rabbi of Conservative rather than Orthodox persuasion. They told the groom to go home and return with the civil marriage license. He protested that this was a distinction without a difference: under New York law, the same rabbi had signed both the civil license and the religious marriage contract. No matter, the official said: "We prefer to recognize the authority granted by the goyim rather than that of the Conservative rabbinate."

This loophole enabling recognition of marriage abroad has been exploited from the first years of statehood, mainly by those deemed by the rabbinate as "forbidden to marry," such as a Kohen marrying a divorcée. Some prominent citizens would rather not be forced to resort to a legal subterfuge but have no other choice.

Haim Cohn, who laid the foundations of Israel's justice system and advocated the adoption of an Israeli constitution, was one of many secular Israelis forced to marry abroad because of the marriage restrictions imposed by the haredi.

One such citizen was Supreme Court Justice Haim Cohen, an outstanding jurist with an Orthodox background, who had to go to New York to legalize his marriage to a woman who had been previously married and divorced. The practice has grown since the 1970s, and increasing numbers of Israelis have gone abroad to circumvent the rabbinical restrictions. A sizable increase in the marriages of Israelis abroad began in the 1990s when the large number of immigrants from the former Soviet Union faced problems while trying to marry at the rabbinate in Israel. Either one or both members of the couple may have had problems proving that they were Jews or had obstacles in their attempts to convert to Judaism. In 1990, nearly three hundred Israeli couples registered for marriage abroad. (Such marriages are commonly called Cyprus Marriages because most of them are held in the neighboring island where the costs are the lowest and the procedure the simplest.) A decade later in 2000, the number of Cyprus Weddings jumped to 3,170 and has continued to rise at a slower rate. In 2007, the number of Cyprus Weddings of Israeli couples was only 5,028.

About three thousand Israeli couples are married each year by Reform and Conservative rabbis in Israel. Since these weddings are not formally recognized by the Israeli rabbinate, a good many of these couples go abroad to obtain a marriage certificate. In addition, each year about four thousand Jewish couples settle for a legal marriage contract prepared by a lawyer. Since an average of fifty thousand Jewish couples decide each year to get married, it is estimated that only 80 percent feel the need to obtain the formal blessing of the rabbinate. While the courts recognize these marital contracts as legally binding in all matters of property ownership, inheritance, and pensions, some difficulties can arise when the children of Covenant Couples want to marry under the rabbinate. The problems created by the religious bureaucracy usually are resolved by a Cyprus Marriage. Jewish couples married by Reform and Conservative rabbis who immigrate to Israel under the 1948 Law of Return must be recognized as Jews if they also have a marriage certificate issued by a civil authority. But in recent years several hundred couples married by Orthodox American rabbis were refused formal recognition of their union because the Israeli rabbinate took sides in the doctrinal and other disputes among American Orthodox rabbis.

The arrival of one million immigrants from the former Soviet Union created a new reality in Israeli life with their speedy absorption in the arts, medicine, politics, and many areas of commerce and industry. That part is an unparalleled success story, but marriage according to religious law presented a barrier: a prudent estimate at the start of the year 2010 was that about three hundred thousand Russian immigrants were unable or unwilling to register with the rabbinate to marry. Many are not deemed Jews according to religious law requiring proof of a Jewish mother, documentation that is not always available to citizens of the defunct Communist state. They were nevertheless eligible to enter Israel under the Law of Return, which requires evidence of only one Jewish parent or even grandparent. To be considered Jewish by the rabbinate, they must undergo a tortuous process of conversion according to Orthodox rules. No doubt some do not want to convert from nominal Christianity, but most likely many more would convert but are put off by the numerous rabbinical obstacles. They would have to promise to raise their children as Orthodox Jews and give them a religious education—obligations that are not demanded of secular Israelis, who are already considered Jews in every respect.

Problems also arise for the Israeli children whose parents were married abroad under civil authority. If even one member of a couple wants to be married in the rabbinate, they encounter barriers. More than once, rabbis have canceled weddings of such couples without appeal or even prior notice. Religious authorities, especially the haredim, argue that if all citizens do not marry under the rabbinate, it would split the Jewish people. They have threatened to create a blacklist of those forbidden to marry—a truly empty threat in a country of six million Jews that is further vitiated by the increase in marriages abroad.

At times a threat has been whispered that the rabbinate would deem children of couples married abroad as bastards. This is frightening but groundless because of definitions of legitimacy in tortuous religious law, which defines as a bastard a child born of incest or a child born to a married woman by a man who is not her husband. But a child born to an *unmarried* woman is considered legitimate—and a woman who has not married in the traditional Orthodox ceremony is not considered married at all. So by that logic, children are safe from the threat of illegitimacy if their mother has married in a civil ceremony abroad. Keeping lists of those "eligible for marriage" may have been effective in the shtetl, the closed Jewish towns of Eastern Europe, but these lists can hardly be enforced in a population from many different traditions, especially with the growing number of those who prefer civil marriages abroad. Thus, even if the rabbinate in one community places hurdles before a young couple, they are likely to find the rabbinate in some other nearby community less inquisitive.

For years coalition partners of the religious parties have suggested solutions to overcome the rabbinical restrictions on registering marriages and granting divorces. One solution that seemed to have good prospects for adoption was put forward in 2004 by the Shinui (Change) Party. Its leaders proposed to create a separate registry for civil marriages that would not diminish the authority of the religious courts over couples who wanted to submit to them. The proposal was written by two Orthodox lawyers who wished to preserve the dominant religious Jewish identity and yet open a way to recognize couples who could not or did not want to register their marriage with the rabbinate. That recognition of civil marriage would have solved the problem of those who nominally lacked a religion, mainly the immigrants who had not undergone an Orthodox conversion. The compromise failed because Shinui, a secular and liberal party that initiated the *brit ha-zugiut* (covenant of the couples), split into feuding factions and vanished from parliament in the next election.

The idea was next taken up by a new party with heavy Russian immigrant support, Israel Beiteinu (Israel Is Our Home), and helped it send a bloc of members to the Knesset in the 2009 elections. One of its conditions for joining in Netanyahu's coalition government was legislation formalizing these covenants; the law would have legitimized civil marriage in fact if not in name. But the religious parties succeeded in blocking the law despite lengthy negotiations. Israel Beiteinu did not carry out its threat to resign from the government but accepted a watered down version of the bill: civil marriage can be registered only when both husband and wife can prove they do not belong to any religion. There are very few, if any, who are eligible for such a marriage, and few have taken place.

Although marriage and divorce are the principal areas of discrimination against women, they are not the only ones. The incident at the dedication of Jerusalem's Calatrava Bridge, where women of the city's dance troupe had to wrap themselves in long skirts and sleeves lest they offend the sensibilities of the local haredim, pales in significance before the historic dispute about equality of the sexes at Jerusalem's Western Wall, the holiest site in Judaism. Until the Jordanian forces conquered the Old City of Jerusalem during the War of Independence in 1948, it was open to both men and women even though the space was confined, and the British police, pressured by Arab nationalists, harassed Jews at prayer. No sooner was the Old City retaken by Israeli forces in June 1967 during the Six-Day War than men and women again came together to pray at the Wall. But after the ramshackle Mugrabi neighborhood next to the Wall was bulldozed to create a large open space for the faithful, the Orthodox rabbinate was granted the administration of Judaism's holiest place, which included the conduct of prayer. The rabbis imposed the separation of the sexes that is normal in Orthodox synagogues, allotting the women a small space to the left of the main prayer area along the Wall for men only. Only after a long struggle by Reform and

Conservative activists were women allowed to conduct their own separate prayers next to the Wall at Robinson Arch, named for the British archeologist who discovered it in the nineteenth century. Joint prayers of men and women are still prohibited there. Secular ceremonies conducted close to the Wall are usually segregated, especially the ceremony of young soldiers taking the oath that starts their military service. When the Jewish Agency conducts a ceremony next to the Wall to award Israeli identity cards to new citizens, men and women are not allowed to stand together. Only at the far edge of the plaza does the rabbinate permit mixed services, such as those for the bereaved families of fallen soldiers on the day before the annual Independence Day.

Another sore point for Israelis seeking equal rights for women is a demand by the haredim for men and women to ride separately on public transport, a type of segregation never enforced in the past. On the contrary, in the interurban *sherut* taxi service men and women travelers have always sat squeezed together. But when the bus cooperative Egged in Jerusalem suggested in 2007 operating a special bus service to take haredim from Meah She'arim to pray at the Western Wall in the Old City it was asked to seat women at the back of the bus. Proud of its "special service," the bus company even gave a name to the segregated buses—Mehadrin, or "Superior."

Egged is a subsidized secular public service and had no authority to enter into agreements in which some clients are separated—even if of their own free will—in preparation for prayer at the Wall. When there was no vociferous public resistance to the separated service to the Wall, Egged consented to introduce separated buses to other locations such as from Meah She'arim to the Orthodox city of B'nai Brak near Tel Aviv and a special service from Ashdod to Jerusalem. In these routes men would enter

Most Israeli synagogues follow the Orthodox tradition separating men and women in prayer. Since the women's section inside the synagogue is usually smaller than the men's, there is often an overflow of women in the courtyard. Note the woman in the center reading from her prayer book, while the women on the right is talking on her phone.

from the front, and women would enter from the middle, filling the seats from the back.

As long as there was no publicity it looked as if the ultra-Orthodox scored another victory. But then the stories of separation of women started making headlines. The Israeli Rosa Parks is a young woman named Tania Rosenblit who boarded a Mehadrin bus in Ashdod on December 17, 2011, and sat behind the driver so that she could be told where to get off in a haredi neighborhood in Jerusalem. When she was told to move to the back of the bus she refused; instead, she took out a camera and started to take photographs of the wild scene that followed. When one of the haredi passengers blocked the door of the bus so the driver could not resume his route, the driver called a policeman. The officer tried to convince Ms. Rosenblit "not to make trouble." After twenty minutes the passengers quieted down and the bus was on its way.

Following this incident six other women complained to the Supreme Court, which ruled that women should not be forced to consent to sit separately on buses but be allowed to sit where they chose. Justice Elyakim Rubinstein opened a loophole for continued separation by explaining his decision: "No operator of public transportation or anybody else should be allowed to tell a woman passenger where to sit anymore than they can tell them what to wear." The haredim drove a bus through the loophole by publishing a picture of a bus with two doors, one in front and one in the back. If women agree to separation by entering through the back door—and social pressure in haredi communities would ensure that—then they can sit separately from the men.

Operators of the Mehadrin service tried to defend themselves by arguing that men and women have long ridden separately on buses in the United States on the regular routes to Manhattan from Orthodox communities in Brooklyn and suburban Rockland County. Egged did not point out that the New York service uses private buses supported by the Orthodox communities themselves, while the Mehadrin service is provided by a publicly subsidized company. But the Israeli Court ruling is not the final word. An inter-ministerial committee appointed by Limor Livnat, the minister of sports and culture, decided several months later to recommend declaring illegal any discrimination against women on public transport and giving drivers special instructions to avoid incidents.

The committee also recommended that the government take steps to stop discrimination against women at funerals, which along with cemeteries have been publicly supported by the gov-

Hundreds of haredim—all men—march together in a funeral procession.

ernment budget since the founding of the state. Orthodox tradition prohibits women from chanting the traditional kaddish prayer at the graveside or even walking with the men in the funeral procession to the cemetery. This tradition may now be ignored if women mourners wish it to be dispensed with.

Efforts to equalize the status of women continue. In July 2009 Rabbi Yuval Sherlo, the head of a yeshiva in Petach Tikva near Tel Aviv, announced proposals to improve the role of women in the synagogue and suggested a committee be formed to do so under Jewish law. He demanded improvement of the women's section in Orthodox synagogues to permit baby carriages during prayers, although he insisted on maintaining a conspicuous *mehitza*, the barrier dividing the men's and women's sections. In synagogues where most of the congregants are graduates of the

Orthodox B'nai Akiva youth movement, there is a growing tendency toward all-*female* minyans, where women chant separately
from the main all-male minyan customary in Orthodox synagogues. Orthodox synagogues still stand firmly against the new
custom of women reading the Torah and prayers in Conservative
and Reform synagogues in parts of Israel. These synagogues attract
many worshippers on the Sabbath and especially on religious hol-
idays. Some have women cantors with beautiful voices and a deep
knowledge of the prayers. Still, these congregations are a minority and often are discriminated against by local authorities that
give preference to Orthodox synagogues.

While the fight for women's equality against the traditions
of Jewish society has intensified, the Jewish mother still holds a
place of honor mainly for her role in the home but remains inferior in public. The most effective way to end the public segregation of women is to avoid its practice: end mandated ritual
baths for betrothed women, enable them to say the kaddish prayer
for the dead alongside male mourners at the graves of their loved
ones, and slowly lift other shameful practices of forced separation.

Most haredi leaders, especially those involved with fund-
raising, know that the segregation of women is the most difficult
practice to defend against their critics. All over the world, including in Israel, women are today an integral part of society. They are
army officers, judges, members of the government, and the backbone of academia. The pitiful attempts to segregate women often
have had the opposite effect from what the rabbis intended. Rigid
separation, in preventing contact between unmarried men and
women, encourages the view of women as sexual objects. If men
and women cannot sit next to each other in school, on a public
bus, or in any other public space, both sexes will only long more
deeply for each other as forbidden fruit.

11

The Sabbath According to Precedent

J UST BEFORE SUNSET ON THE FIRST FRIDAY IN NOVEMBER
of 1969, something unusual happened in Israel. A temporary
injunction issued by Supreme Court Justice Zvi Berenson
allowed television broadcasts to begin on Friday night, just as families across the nation were starting to relax for the weekend. In
Israel such temporary rulings on disputes at the intersection of
religion and society have a way of becoming permanent. More
than forty years later, thanks to the judge's urgent ruling, television shows continue to be broadcast on the Sabbath.

The injunction overturned a decision made by Prime Minister Golda Meir, who had ordered a "temporary" Sabbath ban to
keep her government together following elections just a few days
before. The religious parties had insisted on banning Sabbath
broadcasts as a condition of joining her coalition government. Two
Tel Aviv lawyers challenged the ban, asking the judge to uphold
the Broadcasting Authority's increase in the number of Sabbath
television hours, a decision that had been adopted by a majority

of the authority's board with the deciding vote cast by a foreign ministry official. The government's attorney, Mishael Cheshin, admitted later that he was arguing a weak case with no grounds to overturn the lawful decision of an independent body on the basis of an arbitrary political decision by the prime minister. Later he became a justice of Israel's Supreme Court.

It is difficult to say what would have happened to Sabbath eve TV if not for that Supreme Court injunction. If the fate of supposedly temporary arrangements in other fields is any guide, the ban might have provided a precedent for closing down other kinds of popular entertainment on Friday nights. But once the precedent was established for television, haredi leaders had no choice but to accept political reality, just as it had to accede to public transportation or football games on Saturday afternoons in Haifa because things had always been that way.

But the ultras also won some Sabbath battles. In 1977, El Al, Israel's national airline, had to stop flying anywhere in the world from sundown on Fridays to sundown Saturdays because of political pressure on the ruling Likud coalition, rather than any serious debate on the nature of the Sabbath. This costly curtailment of service was the direct result of the appointment of Avraham Shapira, an Agudat Israel member, as chairman of the Knesset's finance committee. Chubby and disheveled, with his black skull-cap always sliding down his forehead, Shapira was nevertheless a powerful legislator known as Manager of the State because of his great influence on determining facts on the ground. One of them was his success in grounding all planes carrying El Al's livery for one day each week. Never mind the cost (although it was not paid in the way Shapira had foreseen); for the ultra-Orthodox it was a major political victory. The chairman of the finance committee was willing to compensate the airline for the losses incurred by the ban, and even after El Al was privatized in 2004, Sabbath flights were formally prohibited. The new owners preferred to continue receiving the cash compensation to risking a confrontation with the ultra-Orthodox. And furthermore, the airline had already found a way around the ban, so why refuse the subsidy?

As in so many ways in which the haredim claim to have made the Sabbath more holy by prohibiting labor on the biblical day of rest, the real work was performed in erecting a hypocritical curtain of pretense about the so-called Sabbath shutdown. Each Sabbath, El Al runs charter flights under the aegis of a subsidiary, Sun D'or. Passengers who purchase El Al tickets for a scheduled weekday flight departing from Israel can return on Saturday aboard any foreign airline with which El Al has a code-sharing agreement. In fact, Israel's main air terminal, Ben-Gurion Airport, is as busy on Saturdays as any European airport, with flights at all hours of the day not only by Sun D'or but by two Israeli-owned private airlines, Israir and Arkia; only planes carrying El Al markings are grounded for the day. Israel's second busiest airport at the southern tourist playground of Eilat also operates seven days a week. Hundreds of Israeli porters, security guards and inspectors, and officials and technicians at both airports work regular Sabbath shifts.

From the early years of the establishment of the state, the Israeli haredim literally battled for a complete stoppage of all work, as well as public and even private activities. They staged frequent demonstrations that turned violent: they threw stones, burned plastic garbage disposal carts, and fought with the police. The clashes often ended in injuries on both sides as well as arrests. They achieved successes similar to their great victory over El Al. After Bar-Ilan Road, one of Jerusalem's main northern routes, was closed by order of the city's legendary secular mayor Teddy Kollek, an alternative

road connecting West Jerusalem with its eastern and northern sub-
urbs was soon paved to open a way around the Sabbath blockade.

Such minor successes were minor inconveniences in the
lives of most Jerusalemites. But the issue of Sabbath observance
offers the haredim great political leverage in important matters of
state, where they can always threaten to create a coalition crisis to
gain advantage, as they did when they brought down the government on a mere issue of protocol celebrating the untimely arrival
of an American jet fighter. The haredim also shut down rail transport on the Sabbath because the railway company is owned by
the government, but they have been less successful in intimidat-
ing private business and local authorities, where they lack the
leverage afforded by coalition politics.

The tone is more subdued when the target of the protest is a
private or commercial event. Thus, when reporting an invasion of
a hundred black-clad ultras at a football match in Jerusalem in 1960,
the Orthodox newspaper *Hamodea* reported that the teams were
"begged" not to play on the Sabbath. These usually more aggressive
protestors obviously were aware that Israelis prefer attending football games on Saturday and were afraid to antagonize the fans. Some
attempts to pressure Sabbath observance have descended from the
sublime to the ridiculous. During a period of economic austerity
for several years soon after independence, the government decreed
that drivers keep their cars off the streets two days a week to save
imported gasoline. Transport Minister David Zvi Pinkas, a religious
Zionist, tried to kill two birds with one stone by insisting that one
of the two days must be Saturday. This gimmick was met with
public outrage. Amos Keinan, a popular columnist, was accused of
trying to plant an explosive device at Pinkas's door. The journalist
was found not guilty, and in any case the plan to reduce gasoline
consumption was abandoned as impractical.

But the inept attempt to enforce Sabbath observance drew public attention to the campaign by Orthodox politicians to impose restrictions on private life. Pinkas essentially wanted to punish car owners, then a small and relatively privileged group. But many less affluent Israelis still cannot afford to own a car. The only way they can join friends and family on the one day of rest when almost all public transport is banned is to use Israel's fleet of gypsy cabs, known as *sherut*. And spending the biblical day of rest on Israel's magnificent Mediterranean beaches in the summer poses a special inconvenience: drivers have to pay stiff parking fees, and the poor have to walk to and from their homes in the hot sun.

There were other, no less questionable, attempts to impose stricter Sabbath observance in accordance with halacha. Rabbi Yosef Shalom Elyashiv, leader of the "Lithuanians" (noted for their strict interpretation of Jewish law), ruled against Sabbath elevators. These are installed in hotels, hospitals, and some high-rise buildings, operating day and night from Friday to Saturday nights and stopping at every floor; this makes it unnecessary for the rider to press a button to activate the electric motor that, like touching a light switch, is forbidden on the Sabbath. Elyashiv's decision meant that high-rise dwellers might have to walk up ten or more flights of steps—even to attend synagogue—and produced an outcry. (When the revered sage died in 2012 at the age of 102, more than two hundred thousand followers attended his funeral, many of whom undoubtedly lived in high-rise buildings with Sabbath elevators.) In the arguments and counterarguments on Sabbath elevators, an even stricter interpretation of positively Talmudic complexity emerged from one faction—no passing through revolving doors! They argued that those who did so used electricity even if they touched nothing.

What really is at stake in the battle over Sabbath observance is the secular majority's insistence on having its voice heard in the social and cultural debate on how to mark the biblical day of rest. Most Israelis are proud of Judaism's invention of this social achievement, but even secular Israelis want it to be more than an exemption from work. Even in biblical times cows were milked on the Sabbath, and today factories operate seven days a week. Workers are traditionally compensated as they are in all modern economies, by receiving one day off in the middle of the week in exchange for Saturday work. In fact, the behavior of many secular Israelis in observing the distinctive Shabbat ritual is similar to those of more observant citizens—Friday night family dinners, with or without the traditional prayer songs. For many this is the only time during the week when all eat together, including elderly parents and grandchildren.

In secular households, this gathering often includes after-dinner television, which now is as much a part of family life as certain favored dishes at dinner. The extended news broadcasts—Israelis as citizens of an embattled country are news junkies—are followed by cultural programs adjusted to the taste of different audiences; the schedule has become an inseparable part of the experience. Israeli families are dismayed by a nightclubbing culture that has recently sprung up in urban neighborhoods. Too often it leads to brawls and even murders, in large part as a reaction against haredi harassment.

Saturday afternoon football matches have also been a feature of Israeli life since before statehood and therefore were not part of the status quo agreement. Every attempt has failed to move the games to Friday afternoons or midweek. The sport has become increasingly commercialized in Israel as in many other countries, with hundreds of millions invested in the teams. The religious establishment has difficulty in trying to reschedule games

Rabbi Shalom Elyashiv, who until his death in 2012 at the age of 102 was among the extremists of the "Lithuanian" ultra-Orthodox objecting to any modernity, including Sabbath elevators in high-rise buildings

or prevent what they regard as desecration of the Sabbath by fans who arrive at the stadium in their own cars or as part of organized tour groups.

In the early days when Tel Aviv was a small Jewish city before the advent of private cars, the poet Haim Nachman Bialik organized Friday evening cultural programs called Oneg Shabbat (the Pleasure of the Sabbath) at the Ohel Shem auditorium in the city center. But today few halls are suitable for such events: microphones and musical equipment are difficult to operate with automatic Sabbath clocks. So the more that the religious groups insist on all-or-nothing observance, the more secular it becomes in public. Yet even secular Israelis would welcome less traffic in

their neighborhoods on the Sabbath. If some streets with synagogues were shut during the hours of prayer, most drivers would
cooperate by taking alternative routes. What is required is flexibility on both sides, religious and secular.

Sabbath observance in the public domain has increasingly
become subject to the whims of government coalitions and in
fact also to the absolute requirements of modern technology.
When the first high-rise apartment buildings appeared, the hard-
line rabbis led by Rabbi Elyashiv decreed that each must have a
Shabbat elevator to obviate the touch of a button by a religiously
observant human hand. But when the number of these towers
increased, and even began to outnumber the smaller buildings in
many neighborhoods, fewer Sabbath elevators were installed
because they consume more electricity by stopping at every floor
and waste residents' time.

But in accordance with Jewish law, which holds that life is
an overriding value, even the Sabbath may be desecrated to save
a life—the doctrine of *pikuach nefesh*. Who decides what circumstances qualify? In theory, the chief rabbinate has the authority to
do so, but experience has shown that the rabbis are extremely hesitant to issue ordinances. No rabbi would officially deny the need
to maintain a reliable supply of electricity, continued protection by
police and fire-fighting units, and emergency health services. But
few would sign on the dotted line to endorse the need for change.
In reality, precedent rules, determined by practicality. But all too
often the routes around the letter of the law become ridiculous.
The essential argument for avoidance by what is known as the
employment of a Sabbath goy—non-Jews who perform essential
tasks—is that public services must continue to function. But this
is hardly convincing under strict interpretation of the law: the
Bible specifies that work on the Sabbath also applies "to the for-

eigner at your gates." The most ridiculous solution to this dilemma is the Commerce Ministry's choice of inspectors hired from Israel's Druze community—a Muslim sect incorporating elements of Greek philosophy—to hand out tickets to Jewish Sabbath offenders.

In recent years the Sabbath has become one of the most dangerous days of the week for pedestrians and bicyclists because of the increase in private traffic. Drivers who take public transportation all week go to the beach or visit friends in other towns by taking their own cars out of the garage after sundown Friday. On the other hand, while the restful atmosphere is dissipating under haredi pressure, the religious parties' policy of coercion has not served as a barrier to the development of a far less attractive culture of consumerism. Under pressure from developers and secular voters, local authorities have approved huge shopping malls that stay open on Saturdays, now a principal shopping day for many families. Even more objectionable for those who long for the Shabbat rituals of the old days is the official permission for nightclubs and discos to operate on Fridays. Hardly a weekend passes without reports of drunken Friday night brawls in these places, with fistfights, knifings, and an occasional murder.

This deterioration of Shabbat observance is partly an unintended consequence of the haredim's uncompromising interpretation of the Fourth Commandment ("Remember the Sabbath and keep it holy"). They demanded an absolute ban on any public events outside synagogues on Friday, and this has gradually led to the crumbling of all barriers. They began coming down in the usual way, as the unintended consequence of an unexpected minor precedent. In the 1970s, a society of Jerusalem film lovers established a cinematheque to see art films. Friday nights best suited their limited and secular membership, so they fought against a Sabbath ban on such activities and eventually won. Once the barrier was formally lifted for the film buffs, it could not be imposed on other secular activities that were even more objectionable to the haredim—first commercial cinemas, and eventually nightclubs.

However strongly the religious parties object, they cannot function as aggressively as they do at the national level. Municipal councilors have learned that they can lose elections if they try to close down malls or beaches on the Sabbath. Religious politicians have learned from experience that they cannot depend on their representatives in the national government to apply pressure, and that their objections may even backfire. When Jerusalem mayor Nir Barkat decided to open a parking facility on the Sabbath, the haredim demonstrated against it for weeks but could not persuade the ultra-Orthodox representatives in the Knesset to threaten a national political crisis to override the mayor. In a radio interview in July 2009, Yitzhak Pindrus, a Torah Judaism Party representative on the municipal council, made political capital by attacking the haredi extremists for trying to block the parking lot. The haredim also face a dilemma in trying to enforce Sabbath observance: if they employ Jews to check compliance, the Jewish inspectors become Sabbath violators. Hence the welcome Sabbath work for the Druze.

But the religious establishment has scored a victory in achieving the Sabbath closing of restaurants with kosher certification. This is most prevalent in Jerusalem, where restaurants fear losing clients if they cannot certify that they run a kosher kitchen. Nevertheless, there are some loopholes: hotels, which must supply meals to their guests, are allowed to heat the food with equipment that is turned on before the Sabbath, on the assumption that the actual cooking has been completed before sundown Friday.

Even the most zealous kashrut supervisor—which the hotel is obliged to employ—has difficulty distinguishing between a hotel guest who must be served and a diner who walks in and pays for the meal, although not in cash because handling money on the Sabbath is also forbidden.

Another unintended consequence of religious pressure on restaurants to close on the Sabbath is that some chefs reckon they can thrive without the rabbinate's kashrut certificate and stay open on Saturdays because it is a popular day to eat out. This enables them to serve forbidden but popular dishes such as shellfish, pork, and recipes mixing meat and milk. The result is a substantial rise in the number of restaurants serving food that is not kosher—*taref*, literally, unclean. In the center of Jerusalem, where relatively few restaurants are open on Saturday and serve nonkosher food, customers know that they will have to wait for a considerable time for a table in such places.

Professor Yeshayahu Leibowitz, a biologist at the Hebrew University and a meticulous observer of the most obscure religious commandment, was a member of the committee appointed by the chief rabbinate immediately after independence to prepare a Sabbath observance law. Logically such a law would define what is permissible on the day of rest as well as what is forbidden. As a scientist, Leibowitz recognized that no modern society could live without electricity for even one day a week and heaped scorn on the religious establishment for refusing to face up to that fact. But the rabbis did not have the courage to do so and discarded the committee's report. It made no recommendations to the First Knesset and gave no guidance on Sabbath observance. That did not prevent the religious parties from criticizing the government then and now for not enacting a Sabbath law. In 1951, Moshe Unna, a politically liberal Knesset representative from a religious kibbutz, complained that he had received no guidance from the chief rabbinate when laws regulating hours of work and rest were discussed in the labor committee. Instead he heard members of the rabbinate's council sighing that they must have a serious discussion of the problems created by Sabbath observance in a modern society, but no such discussion has ever taken place.

Sixty years have elapsed, and many such questions essential to the operation of a modern economy in a modern state remain unresolved. The inability of the religious circles to propose a Sabbath law that would encompass all aspects of public life has directly and indirectly contributed to the recurring crises. In order to understand what has happened, and why the undesirable aspects of the Sabbath in Israel have become so blatant, it is instructive to recall the case of television broadcasts on Friday nights. Instead of realizinging that such broadcasts could become part of the educational culture of the majority through Sabbath cultural lectures and discussions organized by workers' councils, the haredi minority exerted maximum pressure through its influence in government coalitions. As a result, the possibility of a compromise that would enhance Israeli state television's cultural dimension was lost, to the detriment of modern Shabbat observance and the society as a whole.

12

Sacred Shekels

I F THE CONCEPT OF SIN WERE PART OF JUDAISM, ONE SIN WOULD be making money out of religion. To the great Jewish sages, profiting from the office of rabbi has always been a grave violation of the spirit of Jewish law. "Do not use the Rabbinate as a tool to make a living," wrote the great Maimonides in his twelfth-century commentary on the Mishna. Rabbi Shmaayah, one of the early sages, is quoted in Pirkei Avot (Ethics of Our Fathers): "Love the Craft and hate the Rabbinate." Many others articulated this tradition, which was completely ignored in 2011 by Ya'akov Margi when as minister of religious affairs he awarded stunning raises of 150 percent to most of Israel's rabbis.

Israeli rabbis are appointed for every neighborhood, whether large cities or small communities. Even a village of twenty-five hundred inhabitants is entitled to have a rabbi of its own. All are on the government payroll, supported by the taxpayers. No community can select its own government rabbi, who is a political appointee of the minister of religious affairs. Margi justified the huge salary increases to reduce the gap between junior rabbis and senior rabbis; the latter earn more than 30,000 shekels (about $7,500) a month, roughly the same as a senior hospital doctor.

The press and the public were outraged, but all that the keepers of the nation's public purse could do was shake their heads. "If you want a coalition you have to pay for it," said an official in the Finance Ministry.

But even though they pay their salaries, officials of the Ministry of Religions often have little influence over the egregious acts of some local rabbis. When in 2002 the country was in a state of woe—economic doldrums, terrorism, and political drift—Rabbi David Bazri, a leading cabalist scholar of the Hashalom Yeshiva in Jerusalem, found the reason for the unhappy situation: too many people were masturbating! He called for massive prayers and financial contributions to overcome this evil spirit stalking the nation.

Serving political appointees in the rabbinate and the local religious councils with their large staffs is of course not the only way in Israel to earn a living from religion. Inspecting the observation of dietary laws in the production, serving, and consumption of food is a source of income for tens of thousands of Israelis. It has also spread from food to the unlikely industry of finance. In 2009, thanks to the initiative of another Shas Party member, Deputy Finance Minister Ya'akov Cohen, "kosher" pension schemes were proposed to encourage ultra-Orthodox savers to take their money away from pension managers who did not observe religious law and shift it to companies that did. Cohen said his research indicated that the annual flow of haredi savings and investment totaled about 500 million shekels (about $125 million). He argued that this flow would increase if the haredi savers felt their money was secure in the hands of religiously observant managers.

The issue of setting up pension schemes that would be certified by a rabbinical court was first raised in 2008 with the enactment of a law mandating compulsory savings for retirement, thus compelling the ultra-Orthodox to join the existing schemes. They asked whether they should be permitted to receive pension income from funds invested in companies failing to adhere to halacha. With the creation of pension funds supervised by the rabbinical courts, this question was resolved, at least formally.

There is no way of knowing whether the yield of such "kosher" schemes was higher—or lower—than that of other pension funds. What is incontestable is the fact that tens, if not hundreds, of haredim now have jobs as "kashrut supervisors" of pension funds. Even before Cohen's initiative, religious inspectors were employed by at least ten investment companies. They were drawn from the rabbinical court of the Edah Ha-charedit, the ultras' own supervisory organization that is active in a number of businesses, and the court of Rabbi Aryeh Dvir, the head of the Institute for Economics according to Halacha, a Lithuanian rival of the Hasidic Rabbi Yosef Shalom Elyashiv. Rabbi Dvir awards his seal of approval only upon payment by financial institutions, including the Mercantile Bank, the Mor investment company, and the haredi company Hilat Shoham. The clients of the Edah Ha-charedit rabbinical inspectors include larger companies, such as Excellence-Nesuah, the pension fund Gilad of the Harel insurance company, and Hadas Arazim, which runs its own pension funds. The growth in this financial branch of "kosher supervisors" attracted Rabbi Moshe Yosef, son of the Shas Party leader Rabbi Ovadia Yosef. This outspoken champion of Middle Eastern Jews argues that they must be encouraged to save more for their old age through pension funds, which is also a problem for workers in the United States who have trouble living on their salaries, let alone saving for retirement. So there is no certainty that the increased availability of these rabbinically certified funds would increase the nation's investment pool; most Israelis do not care whether their investments are approved by a rabbinical court and do not regard rabbis as appropriate financial advisers anyway.

How large is this kosher financial sector? The answer depends on how strictly religious laws are observed, and there are numerous loopholes. Bonds of companies paying interest are forbidden, since strict halacha forbids interest. Yet ways have been devised to get around the ban. "Kosher" funds can invest in companies that issue bonds or shares but that decline to deal in unkosher food or operate on the Sabbath. But what of a company that operates to maximize use of its capital and avoid the costs of a weekly shutdown and start-up, like an oil refinery or a manufacturing plant? Such fine distinctions have not been drawn.

Critics of these funds find it a waste of time even to investigate public companies that issue shares, because small shareholders have little if any influence on management in matters such as kashrut or Sabbath observance. They compare this type of single-issue pressure to that of lobbies in Europe that try to organize boycotts of Israeli products or of companies that supposedly assist the Israeli economy. In all these activities there is not a little hypocrisy, recalling the days of the Arab boycott against Israel, which was often subverted by the pure profit motive.

Many more jobs have been created by the guarantee of kosher food, which demands supervisors in farms, slaughterhouses, factories, supermarkets, army camps, and restaurants. This network of employees extends over continents and many countries. Not only does the slaughter of cattle in South American countries provide meat for Israel, but it creates jobs for hundreds of ritual slaughterers and inspectors. Even bottled water from the Italian Alps bears labels attesting to its purity by the Venice rabbinate, which of course charges fees for its certification.

The Passover holiday is an additional source of income for the kashrut supervisors. They place their seal of approval not only on the vineyards (which sell wine all year round labeled "kosher for Passover") but also on soda bottles. Woe to anyone who asks what, if anything, is the danger of food and drink that is not kosher for Passover finding its way into a soda bottle. Everyone pays and few question the practice. After cattle and fowl are slaughtered, and food is produced in factories under supervision, inspectors in groceries and restaurants levy their tariff on this final link in the food chain. This group is usually the only one visible to the consumer of kosher food.

The 1983 law against kashrut fraud empowers the chief rabbinate, the army rabbinate, and rabbis they recognize to grant certificates of kashrut. But in places that produce food or serve it, supervisors are appointed by the local rabbinate, and more often than not, these supervisors are paid by the owner of the enterprise—a clear conflict of interest and indication of the lack of rigor in observing the dietary laws. In mid-2009 State Controller Micha Lindenstrauss issued a report criticizing the chief rabbinate and the food industry for allowing a network of kashrut supervisors to operate outside the direct oversight of the rabbinate and answer not to the rabbis, but to the enterprises that paid the supervisors on their own premises. The controller also reported that the supervisors did not work according to written standards, and examinations did not even exist to test their competence.

Six months passed after the state controller issued his report until Margi publicly agreed that the criticism was justified, thanked him for his report, and proceeded to put it into effect. Henceforth kashrut supervisors would have to pass examinations. They would not be paid by food establishments but by manpower companies operating on the model of independent security companies, which would also hire them in place of local rabbis, who were subject to pressure from politicians and relatives.

From time to time the rabbinate has pushed against the exceptions for restaurants and hotels operating on the Sabbath and sought to broaden its own prohibitions. What is the rule for a Sabbath meal at a wedding hall after a Reform rabbi has married the couple? Can a restaurant be denied a kashrut certificate because the owner travels on the Sabbath? Some local rabbis have refused to allow weddings in a hotel that does not have a Sabbath elevator. The civil courts have pushed back against such rabbinical encroachments, and in 1990 Supreme Court Justice Theodor Or overturned a rabbinical denial of kashrut to a restaurant. The judge ruled that a certificate could be denied only if the food itself was not kosher.

Since the kashrut industry employs thousands of supervisors and middle men, it is not surprising that many competitors have invaded this lucrative business. Ostensibly the law gives the monopoly to the chief rabbinate, but since the haredim have never recognized its authority over this domain, the ultras have initiated a full-fledged kashrut inspection service of their own. So have several other groups. As a result, every producer and distributor of food can choose from eight or more inspection services, with the chief rabbinate seeking to oppose its rivals, but too weak to do so, so that many employers are unaware that it is supposed to have a monopoly over enforcing kashrut.

That has made the Edah Ha-charedit, the religious inspectorate of the haredim, the competitor of the rabbinate's supervision network. Others have occupied this legal limbo, so that today there are at least ten more religious inspectorates that owe their existence to that of the Edah Ha-charedit. Some of the smaller organizations were created against the background of disputes over obscure points of religious law, with the adherents of one group refusing to accept the decision of another. Thus there is the Bet Yosef inspectorate of Rabbi Ovadia Yosef's Shas Party, the Hatam Sofer in B'nai Brak, the Mahzikei Hadas of the Beltz Hasidim, the Yoreh De'ah of Rabbi Shlomo Mahpour, and so on. Sometimes a religious inspectorate is created when it has assured itself in advance of a large number of adherents, thus justifying its existence. An example of this is She'erit Yisrael of the Degel Ha-torah Party, among whose clients are numbered Strauss's salad and vegetable divisions, the Angel bakeries in Jerusalem and Ramle, and the Crystal label drinks produced by Yaffa-Tavori.

Occasionally the business link between a kashrut inspectorate and a client seeking its services is so blatant that it can no longer be ignored. Rabbi Ovadia Yosef's picture appeared on the calendar distributed by the Israeli franchisee of Denmark's Carlsberg beer company, which received its certificate from his Bet Yosef inspectors. Not surprisingly, the Shas Party also supported an appeal by the local Carlsberg company to levy a deposit on bottles of more than one liter, conveniently exempting Carlsberg's smaller bottles.

Usually it is thought that the certification of a rabbinical organization is reliable and even more stringent that of the rabbinate itself, akin to the distinction between kosher and "glatt kosher." This is a technical distinction deriving from the state of the lungs of a slaughtered animal but is actually a distinction without a difference, although it has been adopted to cover all foods as a sort of reassurance—for which the consumer must pay extra. The Badatz Haedah Ha-charedit, the ultra-Orthodox organization, competes against the kashrut departments of the local rabbinates, while the smaller organizations compete among themselves. For once, this competition benefits the consumer;

shoppers can be seen in supermarket aisles checking to see whether the rabbinical inspectorate they prefer is named on the package. Unfortunately, only the religious consumer benefits rather than the secular housewife, who must pay for the extra kashrut certification on every loaf of bread and every bottle of mineral water whether or not it matters to her or her family. This cost is in addition to the taxes paid to support government and local authorities that finance all the arms of the rabbinate as well as the education of thousands of students in the yeshivot.

Sometimes the strict observance of kashrut can be combined with discrimination against women in ridiculous ways. A restaurant called Heimish Essen ("Home Cooking" in Yiddish) serves East European dishes in Jerusalem's secular neighborhood of Rechavia; the waiters had long included modestly dressed women, and kashrut was observed under strict supervision of Badatz belonging to the Agudat Israel Party. But in 2012 the Badatz ruled that on Thursday nights (called "Friday Eve" in haredi vernacular) only men would be allowed to serve food. The ruling was based on the fact that on Thursdays many of the diners are yeshiva students who have the evening off and do not want to be served by women. The infuriated owner of the restaurant argued that the kashrut of the food had no connection with the sex of the waiters and encouraged his secular waiters to demonstrate in front of the restaurant. Unfortunately, he lacked the courage to dump the Badatz as his kashrut supervisors and take his business to inspectors with less strict demands.

When the Shinui Party was in the government, it celebrated its first victory by dismantling the Ministry of Religious Affairs and transferring responsibility for services to local authorities. But the triumph was short-lived. Over the years, a dense layer of wasteful and corrupt officials had accumulated inside the ministry, and this patronage could not be eliminated without threatening the collapse of the governing coalition. That prompted its revival under the name of the Ministry for Religious Services, although its costs for kashrut supervision, religious services, and construction and maintenance of synagogues—40 million shekels, or about $10 million—are marginal compared to the outlay on schools for haredi children. But buried in the budget for religious services are some strange provisions. The minister, Ya'akov Margi, complained that the 160,000 shekels (about $40,000) allotted by the Finance Ministry to string wires and create an *eruv* (a marker delineating an area in which strict observers of the Sabbath are allowed to carry small packages) was inadequate because the real cost would be ten times larger. If Israelis were polled on who needed an *eruv* and even what it was, probably no more than one in ten would favor the posts and wires connecting them to a place of worship. The devices are honored only by the Orthodox but end up on the bill of every taxpayer instead of the local authorities, who are supposed to underwrite religious services.

The budget is much larger for building separate neighborhood synagogues for each ethnic group. Many ask whether there is still a need in every town, large or small, for separate Ashkenazi and Sephardic rabbis after decades of coexistence between the two branches. And why must the government budget bear the expense of 600,000 shekels (about $150,000) for a mobile *mikvah* for the Orthodox community of Amatziah and a bath for men only in the West Bank settlement of Elon Moreh? Rachel Azaria, a young member of Jerusalem's municipal council, was astounded shortly after her election to learn that parents of children in kindergartens for the general public pay 70 percent of the expenses and the municipality 30 percent, mostly for aid to those in poorer neighborhoods, while in haredi kindergartens the proportion is reversed because so many of the ultra-Orthodox live at or below the poverty line. In the school system as a whole, the weight of payment falls even more heavily on the parents of secular pupils.

Although rabbis have long been appointed and their salaries fixed by the ministries of religion under their various names, the money is disbursed by the local authority in which they serve. However, the money is all too often diverted to other municipal purposes. Nevertheless, they must perform their appointed tasks, such as wedding ceremonies for couples who live within the town boundaries. Many of these rabbis also charge additional fees, claiming expenses for taxis and other incidentals. In September 2009 a joint committee of the Ministry of Justice, the chief rabbinate, and the Ministry for Religious Services decreed—and not for the first time—that rabbis paid by local and regional authorities could not accept a fee for performing a marriage ceremony if the bride or groom lived in the district. The committee had discovered that most rabbis demanded between 200 and 400 shekels (about $50 to $100), and some received thousands for performing this mitzvah—the more prominent the rabbi, the higher the payment he expected. Even though the decision prohibiting a fee to a public official for officiating at a wedding seems logical, it was arrived at only after prolonged discussion that included such extras as the rabbi's travel expenses (to be paid by the couple's family). Since the rabbis are civil servants, the committee determined that a rabbi can perform services outside his regular duties only with the permission of his superiors and must report to them every six months on his private work, which is subject to a specified number of hours in any given day.

As the proportion of ultra-Orthodox increases, so does the burden on the local authorities because they are financed almost entirely by property taxes, and the income from haredi property is negligible. This problem is especially acute in Jerusalem, where the haredim constitute one-third of the population and their share of property tax payments is almost nonexistent. In 2009 an attempt was made to obtain some income from haredi families by levying water charges, labeled a "drought tax." A haredi delegation appeared before the Knesset Finance Committee to plead for a postponement to September so families with many children would not suffer during the hot summer months. The committee was headed by a rabbi and compromised on a delay until August. But the minimum quantity at which the tax kicked in was simultaneously increased to favor water quotas for families of more than five persons.

This special tax rate for haredi families was only one of many suggestions designed to mitigate their poverty. Deputy Finance Minister Cohen had another idea to ease the distress of his Shas voters: to have his ministry pay the premiums of policies insuring the lives of older yeshiva students, most of whom are fathers of families. The government-supported yeshivot are supposed to pay the premiums that many could not afford, and Cohen tried to come to their rescue. He was publicly opposed by Alon Unian of Israel's Givat Washington College, one of the institutions that tries to train the haredim for productive work. Unian argued that additional subsidies only made it easier for these adult students to avoid employment and urged Cohen's ministry to invest the money in scholarships for yeshiva students to learn a trade.

Israelis have reluctantly tolerated this petty corruption for years: if rabbis performing their sacred duties do not merit some special privileges in the Jewish state, then where should they? But there are signs that this tolerance is reaching a limit, and the sharpest evidence is not seen directly but in the political crisis over the issue that touches every Israeli citizen—religious or secular, strictly kosher or not—universal military service and the exemption granted to the students and followers of the haredim. On closer examination, this exemption is an essential pillar of the hyper-observant society they have created, elements of which they seek to impose on other Israelis. Once the haredi youth are thrown in with others of their generation, many are unlikely to be content to remain in an isolated minority among their fellows, and the barriers to assimilation erected by their rabbis will surely weaken if not actually fall.

Such social changes take time, and even the Kadima leaders were willing to settle for a four-year transition period toward a universal draft. But the expiration of the Tal Law opened the haredi youth to assimilation in another less obvious and possibly more rapid way. When the law expired, it was not replaced by anything else, and the end of the legal military exemption for the yeshiva students also ended the legal basis for the government allowances they receive for *not* performing military service. Without these allowances, the economic basis of their lives changes radically, since most come from poor families. And will they be such loyal soldiers of the haredi army when they are no longer paid to serve?

Several citizens groups appealed to the Supreme Court to resolve the issue, which the Netanyahu government sidestepped by ruling that the allowances will be paid "temporarily." But rather than settling into a kind of permanence like originally temporary Sabbath television, the costly allowances are more likely to become just as much of a political flashpoint as the military exemption itself. No one can say how much of the rest of Israel's overbearing religious superstructure will survive that political battle, which the haredim could take into the streets.

1 3

The Changing Nature of Jewish Solidarity

I N THE LAST MONTHS OF 2009, SEVERAL THOUSAND VIOLENT young ultra-Orthodox demonstrators flooded into the streets of Jerusalem on Saturdays to protest Sabbath work at Intel, the international electronics giant producing computer chips at its big local plant. The demonstrations soon began following a weekly routine. Each ended with several rioters and policemen wounded and some rioters arrested, followed by their release within a day or two. Then, after several weeks, the demonstrations ended as inexplicably as they had begun. So what had Intel done, and why the protests now?

The organizers not only knew that chip production requires an uninterrupted manufacturing process but that it had been under way ever since the plant went into production almost two decades before. This sudden discovery of Intel's "desecration of the Sabbath" was curious indeed: why did the young haredim single out this respected multinational rather than direct their wrath at the dozens of bars and nightclubs, where the drink-fueled Sabbath revelries spilling into the street on Friday nights are certainly far more objectionable than the sober Saturday work shift at Intel. One possible explanation, rumored at the time, was that the rioters, students of Toldot Aharon (History of Aaron), a well-known yeshiva in the Meah She'arim quarter of Jerusalem, were ordered to assist in its ambitious fund-raising campaign then under way in the United States. They probably were told that a spirited demonstration would certainly impress potential benefactors in New York with their highly motivated defense of the sanctity of the Sabbath.

The demonstrators were counting on Jewish solidarity in its original form, which is essentially charitable. Throughout the ages, this has taken many forms, including the support of Jews expelled from their homes; the Jewish refugee aid organizations such as the Hebrew Immigrant Aid Society (HIAS) and the Joint Distribution Organization are the prime examples in our day. Even before the Zionist awakening, religious Jews began arriving in the Holy Land in the mid-nineteenth century. When the first groups of the ultra-Orthodox arrived mainly from Lithuania and Galicia, these pious Jews expected their Diaspora brothers to support them. In their own profound belief as well as that of Jews abroad, they were performing an important role by settling in the Holy Land, praying for the souls of Jews everywhere, and devoting their lives to the study of Talmud. It was as if they were saying kaddish—the prayer honoring the souls of the dead—on behalf of those who supported them from the great commercial cities of New York, London, and Warsaw. It was almost a give-and-take agreement between the two groups.

Whether the riots in Jerusalem actually took place in close coordination with an ultra-Orthodox fund-raising campaign in America, the fact remains that of the $1.5 billion in charitable contributions that flow into Israel from abroad each year, less than one-quarter of the funds are directed to the haredim. Before the

Extremists belonging to the Toldot Aharon Hassidic sect clash with Israeli police. They objected to the production of microchips at Intel's Jerusalem plant on the Sabbath.

Zionist immigration, things were different. When the first ultra-Orthodox, known as the Old Yishuv, arrived in the Holy Land from Europe in the mid-nineteenth century, they claimed to have made the arduous journey to Jerusalem not only for themselves but to speed the arrival of the Messiah and pray for all Jews everywhere. Thus they were doing them a mitzvah—performing good and moral deeds on their behalf, for which of course they expected help and support. The systems of raising money from

193

abroad were varied but also tried and true, and there was no need to make any major changes over the years.

First the Shadarim (the Hebrew acronym for Shilichim Derabanan, or Emissaries of the Rabbis) were sent out to the Jewish communities of the Diaspora, lecturing mainly at synagogues to describe the hard life they led in Jerusalem and playing on the conscience of their more prosperous brethren. Naturally, these Shadarim kept a sizeable part of what they collected as their commission and to pay their expenses. Then there were the letters—an active trade in the addresses of potential contributors among the various institutions of learning and welfare, pioneers in what we now call direct mail. Once they had compiled a lengthy mailing list, letters were composed describing the poverty of the pious suppliants and explaining the important service they were performing to world Jewry. Alas, they were so poor that they had no money to buy paper or envelopes, or to pay for printing the letters, let alone buy the postage stamps. So even they were purchased on credit. Before 1917, when Palestine was part of the Ottoman Empire, there were competing postal services—Russian, Austrian, and German, as well Turkish. Some were only too eager to attract business by offering stamps on credit. As the replies arrived, the postal clerks slit open the envelopes before forwarding them and collected their debts.

Some of this kind of fund-raising continues, especially appeals by mail to unknown addressees. But what has drastically changed, however, is the proportion between the huge pool of potential contributors abroad and the tiny colony of the needy in their holy outpost of Jerusalem. In the nineteenth century, more than ten million Jews lived and worked in Europe and the United States, and most were Orthodox or at least observant; today there are over six hundred thousand haredim in Israel, many of them needy in part because they follow a life of study and not work. The Israeli ultras do not seem to be disturbed by seeking contributions from all Jews abroad, including their Reform and Conservative brethren who are regularly condemned in Israel's haredi synagogues as heretics.

As long as Israeli haredim can appeal to Jews abroad on the basis of their physical needs, or seek help against interference by the secular government with their observance of Jewish traditions, they will obtain the support and financial contributions from Jews abroad, even from those who lead a secular life. However, when the haredim in Israel engage in activities that are odious to Jews abroad, such as the separation of men and women on public transportation, the reaction is mostly negative and the haredim must close ranks to protect their supporters abroad. Under Israeli law, voluntary societies seeking tax exemptions must register and disclose their contributors unless granted special permission, for example, to seal off their lists of donors from other fund-raisers. At least half of the sixteen organizations granted this exemption of secrecy are dedicated to haredi causes. By contrast, television, with its immediate coverage of events thousands of miles away, has a much stronger impact on a worldwide audience than the Shadarim of the olden days or the emotional speakers begging, cajoling, and shaming foreign Jews to support the struggling Jewish state in its early years.

But an embattled Israel nevertheless can attract money from American Jews. The Cohen Institute at Brandeis University found that, adjusting for inflation, private U.S. contributions doubled between 1994 and 2007, when they reached $2.1 billion. Donations grew most slowly to ultra-Orthodox education (most haredi fund-raising is conducted under the rubric of education) and totaled $120 million. Thus the haredim received only 5 percent of

American Jewish donations to Israel and therefore have been forced to become heavily dependent on the Israeli government for financial support.

Since the Brandeis survey, American aid to the haredim has most likely deteriorated even more as a result of their bad press in the United States. In 2011 the *Washington Post* columnist Ruth Marcus, in an article titled "In Israel, an Unequal Life for Women," compared discrimination against Saudi Arabian women under Muslim sharia law with incidents in Israel, a point picked up within a few days by Secretary of State Hillary Clinton. A widely published photograph of haredi boys spitting on a nine-year-old girl as she walked to school without stepping off the sidewalk in Beit Shemesh caused widespread disgust in America. In reporting the U.S. military raid that killed Osama bin Laden, an Orthodox newspaper in Brooklyn airbrushed out the figures of all the women, including Mrs. Clinton, that appeared in the original photograph of President Obama and his national security team anxiously awaiting the outcome in the White House Situation Room. Although it was circulated and printed around the world, the editors were ridiculed in Israel as well as America for bowdlerizing it, as well as for their explanation that some readers might be offended by the images of women. Newspapers circulating in the American Jewish community also featured the story of Tania Rosenblit's troubles on the Mehadrin bus. Such incidents did more to turn off Americans from sympathizing with Israeli Orthodoxy than any number of carefully reasoned speeches and articles. Likewise, there was incomprehension and disgust when a group of Jerusalem haredim put yellow Stars of David on their clothes to dramatize their supposed persecution in Israel. The general impression left by these and other stories was quite the opposite of that intended by the haredi demonstrators. They conveyed accurately the impression that discrimination against women and the separation between the sexes in ultra-Orthodox communities were not isolated incidents but part of an accepted way of life.

Were the Israeli haredim a self-sufficient community living apart from their Jewish brethren, such behavior might be tolerated and even understood by anyone familiar with biblical accounts of the role of Jewish women. But their dependence on Jews abroad has turned them into beggars (*shnorers* in popular Yiddish), although after the outbursts of 2011 they appear to have curbed their worst excesses in "mixed society" and limited them to their own tight-knit community.

American researchers at the Floersheimer Institute estimate that there are at most four hundred thousand ultra-Orthodox Jews living in the Borough Park, Crown Heights, and Williamsburg sections of Brooklyn, and perhaps another hundred thousand scattered elsewhere in the United States. Ultra-Orthodox communities in Britain, Canada, France, Switzerland, and Belgium (mainly in Antwerp's diamond district) add up to perhaps another hundred thousand. While on average the American Orthodox Jew may be less affluent than more secular American Jews, they are closely connected to their fellow Israeli haredim and devoted to their welfare. The principal difference between the two groups lies in education and occupation. Most of the American ultra-Orthodox Jews have studied English, mathematics, and science in Jewish or public schools, as required by law. Nevertheless, they find no contradiction between their modern educational accomplishments and the concentration on Jewish studies by the Israeli haredim. Indeed, some send their own children for periods of study in Israeli yeshivot to absorb the language, culture, and traditional ways.

A few American and British haredim do insist on courses of purely Jewish studies for their children and send them to an Israeli

Talmud Torah or yeshiva where they not only are exposed to a thorough haredi atmosphere but often are not charged tuition. This is illegal under Israeli law since the government allocates its subsidy to each institution according to its number of students; the administrators of the yeshivot therefore are not eager to distinguish between Israeli and foreign students.

The American haredim in Brooklyn and in Rockland County, north of New York City, resemble their Israeli brethren in their dress, in their strict observance of religious rules, and in their insistence on marriage within the group. The broad-brimmed black hats and the fur hats worn on the Sabbath and festive occasions symbolize an attempt to maintain in America, just as in Israel, the traditional dress and social structure of earlier centuries in Eastern Europe. But the Brooklyn haredim, aware that their children cannot count on government welfare, offer a basic education following the state curriculum. A far smaller proportion of their sons attend yeshivot after high school, and those who do so tend to study for fewer years than those in Israel.

The best known among American haredim is the large Hasidic sect of Chabad, which has its headquarters at 777 Eastern Parkway in the Crown Heights section of Brooklyn. The sect, also known as the Lubavitchers, is named after the Russian town that was its headquarters for almost two hundred years. The sect was founded in the late eighteenth century by Rabbi Shneior Zalman, whose book the *Tanya*—meaning "we learned" in Aramaic—is based on elements of the mystical study of the cabala: Chochma, Bina, and Da'at, from which is derived the Hebrew acronym Chabad that gives the sect its official name. Today it counts about two hundred thousand adherents, most in New York and Israel, and they are active and visible in proselytizing. During the last sixty years, especially when headed by its charismatic leader, the late Menachem Mendel Schneerson, Chabad adopted a missionary zeal mobilizing its members and their supporters all over the world. Chabad now has about four thousand centers spread over 950 cities and towns in seventy-five countries. In countries like India, Nepal, and Thailand, the Chabad centers have also attracted tens of thousands of Israeli backpackers for meals and a place of worship and comfort. The Chabad center in Mumbai, India, was a target of the murderous attack of Pakistani-based terrorists who killed its rabbi, his wife, and ten of their guests. Undeterred, the Chabad reopened and recently has extended to a site in China near the old Jewish colony in Shanghai.

Even before other haredi movements became involved in Israeli politics, Chabad supported right-wing Israeli parties and came out against giving up "parts of the historic Land of Israel." In this respect Chabad does not differ from several other American Jewish organizations, which during the last decade have been driven to support Israel's right wing in order to maintain their connection and control over their increasingly conservative membership base. This also influences American politics, which, with the further support of the Christian evangelical right, has been hesitant to apply U.S. pressure against Israeli expansionism. The American Jewish writer Peter Beinart has noted that most American Orthodox Jews now support the Israeli right, and some even extend their support to extremists such as Rabbi Dov Wolpe, who urges Israelis not to rent apartments to their fellow countrymen if they happen to be Arabs. This rightward shift arises from the secularization of educated American Jews, increasing numbers of whom tend to marry outside the faith; this cools their interest and support for Israel, weakening classic Jewish solidarity. As a result, the American Jewish establishment has had to redirect its energies and concentrate its search for support among the

Orthodox and even the ultra-Orthodox in America. In the process Jewish leaders have shifted their support to the policies of Israel's nationalist right, a phenomenon fully understood and exploited by Netanyahu. Chabad has openly intervened in Israeli election campaigns, and some extremists finance Israel's lunatic fringe, but most support, including campaign donations by American right-wing Jews, goes to Netanyahu's Likud Party. This indirectly helps him resist some of the more outrageous demands of the haredi parties, but it also stiffens his resolve against formal negotiations with the Palestinian leadership for a two-state solution in the former territory of Palestine.

Such findings raise two important questions about the involvement and especially the awareness of American Jews. What percentage of American Jewry actively supports the activities of the ultra-Orthodox, who are a very small minority among American Jewry and almost as small a segment of the Israeli population? Most American Jews support Israel as a broad-based Zionist project, a homeland for all Jews (and in the minds of many, a potential refuge in dark times). Support comes through synagogues (including Reform and Conservative congregations celebrating the traditional rituals in forms that are reviled by the haredim), broad-based Zionist organizations, and local chapters of the B'nai B'rith. The descendants of the Old Yishuv are no longer a priority. Since the start of the new millennium, financial support by the U.S. Reform movement to Israeli congregations has decreased considerably, with donors claiming budgetary shortcomings at home. The largest donations flow to hospitals and educational organizations such as the Hadassah and Sha'areri Tzedek hospitals in Jerusalem and to Israel's three main universities.

Few American Jews are aware of the internal strife among Israelis over the role of the Orthodox rabbinical establishment and its political influence. Nevertheless, most of the financial support for haredi causes in Israel comes not from ultra-Orthodox families but from contributors who are expressing a nostalgic if ill-informed sympathy for the idea of the yeshiva passing on "Jewish learning." It seems more likely that if the recipients of the many appeals for donations to haredi institutions were aware that graduates are not prepared for productive work by those very yeshivot and that rabbinical courts blatantly discriminate against women, donors would most likely be much less generous.

Israel is a small country, but like America it was founded on a commonly accepted ideology and, at least until recent times, was governed by compromise among groups via a common language through a process that is known in both countries as a melting pot of immigrants. Israel's internal struggles sound a warning for America: a disciplined and determined minority that is confident of divine favor can win its own way, splinter a democratic government, and in time wear down the democratic process. Fundamentalist religion is anathema to any modern society, and the test of strength now under way in Israel is also taking place in America between secular politicians and evangelical Christians. It is no accident that the religious groups in both countries are allied in part by their views on the role of religion in civil society. The political conflict over military service in Israel also proves they can be a powerful threat.

At one time, particularly in the years immediately after the 1967 Six-Day War, things were different. At that time support for Israel came from young Jews at university and liberal and secular intellectuals. They were impressed by the pioneering spirit in the collective settlements and admired the splendid young men and women who, once and for all, proved that Jews could rise up and defend themselves. Nobody mentioned the thousands who enter yeshiva instead of putting on their country's uniform. Today young Jewish students have joined anti-Israel movements on campus to protest the conduct of the West Bank occupation and occasionally demonstrate against spokesmen defending Israeli government policy. To counter these trends, projects such as Taglit (Birthright) bring thousands of young men and women from America and Europe each year for short visits to Israel that are packed with emotion in reinforcing their Jewish identity, but also build political support for expansionist policies and religious practices that they would not tolerate at home.

Some social scientists believe that the special relations with Jews abroad and their financial support of Israel, especially of the haredi community, will eventually weaken to nostalgia like the sentimental ties of Italian, Polish, and other immigrants cummunities for their mother land. This loosening of deep spiritual attachments will become more evident as the gap increases between the majority of American Jews who belong to Reform and Conservative congregations and the ultra-Orthodox movement in Israel they are asked to support. As Beinart correctly observed, the Israeli leadership has already become aware of these trends and is trying to maintain the bond with American Jews by appealing to nationalistic sentiments and right-wing slogans. When Netanyahu, in his speech to the AIPAC (American Israel Public Affairs Committee) delegates in 2012, used photos demonstrating the U.S. refusal to bomb the Auschwitz death camp in 1944, he well knew he was appealing to one of the lowest common denominators between American Jews and Israel. Will American support for the Israeli haredim dwindle? This depends largely on the behavior of haredi groups in America like Chabad. If its popular appeal declines, its outposts in Israel will no doubt feel the blow.

1 4

How Will the War End?

IN A RARE INTERVIEW THAT REQUIRED COURAGE AND REFLECTED a mood that prevails privately among ultra-Orthodox in Israel, a young man identified only by his nickname, Yanky, spoke early in 2012 to a reporter for *Ynet*, a popular Israeli Internet news service. He is one of tens of thousands of haredi youngsters living in disguise. Like all haredi men, Yanky wears only black slacks and a coat over his long-sleeved white shirts, his head covered by a broad-brimmed felt hat—a thoroughly uncomfortable costume in the climate of the Middle East. The haredi women and even young girls wear dresses long enough to reach to their ankles. These male and female haredi uniforms were clearly imported from Europe with one purpose in mind: to bind followers to rabbinical leadership and supervision and separate them from the rest of their fellow citizens. Just as their fear that military service will tug their youth toward secular pursuits and away from the suffocating embrace of the haredi community, ordinary street dress may work a similar influence. Anyone wearing this somber uniform, as well as a long beard, will not dare to enter a bar or restaurant that is not totally kosher on pain of immediate recognition by other patrons. Their antique dress separates all members of the haredi community from the secular world. But it also intensifies its internal conflict and individual frustrations.

Yanky admitted that his attire, his black suit, his Sabbath fur hat known as a *shtreimel*, and his long beard were in fact just a masquerade. He was just a make-believe haredi, as if he were dressed for the popular Purim holiday. In private, he said, he often turns on the electric light on the Sabbath and sometimes even mixes meat and milk dishes in one meal. Yanky told the reporter that he belonged to a growing group of pretenders who call themselves Haredi Maranos after the Jews in Spain who posed as Christians in order to escape the wrath of the Inquisition. He and his fellow Maranos no longer felt obliged to lead the secluded life of strict orthodoxy and yeshiva studies. At the same time, they lack the courage for an open revolt against the strict society that raised and sheltered them. His frustration intensified after he was ordered to marry at the age of nineteen, and social pressure forced him into the yeshiva full-time. He was appalled at the strict and often hypocritical discipline imposed by the rabbis and especially by their fanatical attachment to sites presumed to be tombs of biblical saints, which in fact were tombs of Muslim sheikhs from recent centuries.

In a popular evening television talk show, a bearded young man not unlike Yanky told of his "unusual" rabbi, whom he consulted before traveling to the Galilee to pray at the tombs of ancient rabbinical heroes. To his surprise the rabbi told him: "For this purpose you do not have to travel from Jerusalem to the Galilee. Just go by bus to Mount Herzl right here, where so many of our soldiers who fell in Israel's recent wars are buried. There you will find many, many holy heroes!"

Yanky has neither the courage nor the means to move to a part of Jerusalem where he can dress as he wishes and teach his children to follow his version of Judaism without risking the condemnation of his neighbors. We will probably learn the size of this group of secret Maranos only when and if the war within approaches some kind of resolution. There can probably never be a decisive end. No modern society can govern itself exclusively by either faith or reason; the two poles must bend toward each other. The struggle between Israel's secular society and its ultra-Orthodox minority for control of the country's destiny will no doubt continue. Some in Israel even foresee a creeping victory of the halacha as the norm of the state, and the eventual conversion of Israel into a theocratic democracy. The regime of Iran and the rise of the Islamist parties following the Arab Spring in Tunisia and in neighboring Egypt seem to foreshadow similar religious pressures in Israel. Disappointed by modernism and corruption, the groups in neighboring Middle East countries have accepted the leadership of religious oligarchs while maintaining a nominally democratic government.

Among Israeli scholars the most outspoken in the belief that the advance of the haredim cannot be checked is Nachman Ben-Yehuda, a Hebrew University professor of sociology who compiled a database of newspaper reports about the ultra-Orthodox. It covers the first half century of Israel's independence. In his book *Theocratic Democracy: The Social Construction of Religious and Secular Extremism*, Ben-Yehuda finds no evidence of compromise. He foresees continued stalemate leading to what he calls "creeping halacha"—a slow but inevitable advance of the rule of religious law in Israel, similar to what is taking place in other countries in the Middle East.

He bases his analysis not only on the continuous gains of the ultrareligious in obtaining their demands from the majority through financial subsidies, but on their quick resort to violence. Extremist groups like the students of the Toldot Aharon yeshiva (the demonstrators against the Intel factory whose production continues through the Sabbath) impose their will on other ultra-Orthodox groups with no less ferocity than they display in their confrontation with the Israeli police. Professor Ben-Yehuda argues that even when they fail—as they did in trying to prevent a Jerusalem parking lot from operating on the Sabbath—these religious zealots will simply try again, a year of two later, until they succeed. After all, it took them almost thirty years (and a right-wing government) to force El Al to ground its planes on the Sabbath.

He also finds a resemblance between the haredi quest for a theocratic state and the struggle for a Greater Israel by the settlers on the West Bank. Granted, the two groups started from different ideologies and use different tactics. While the haredim ground their belief in the arrival of the Messiah, the religious Zionists—who since 1967 have become more strict in their observance of religious law—believe the Messiah will come only when the Jews themselves bring him by strengthening and expanding their state. What are the chances (or dangers, as many secular Israelis see it) that Israel will move in this direction, either by the growing force of the haredim or by an unwritten alliance with religious Zionists? The story of Yanky and his Maranos may be just one indication that the ultra-Orthodox camp is not as formidable as its political accomplishments have made them appear.

In fact, since Ben-Yehuda compiled his database, the haredim have changed their tactics to promote their cause and gain the goodwill of secular society. Instead of displaying their wrath by Sabbath riots, clashes with the police, and the burning of plastic garbage containers, they have chosen to speak more softly in a mode known in Judaism as *darchei noam*—routes of pleasantness. These include an attempt to explain their way of life in a popular television series and support for an exhibition on the

Hasidic tradition at the Israel Museum in Jerusalem. The exhibition stressed the elegant behavior and dress of men and women among generations of Hasidic leaders, and the different sects' beautiful gold and silver artifacts, cups and glasses used in the synagogues, and dining tables. Representations of the jumbled haredi neighborhoods in modern Israel and their antecedents in the poverty-stricken village shtetls of Eastern Europe were nowhere to be seen. Nor was there any hint of the hidden tension between the generations over the future of the young when confronted with the attractions as well as the demands of the secular world.

There has been a slight change in the attitude of some *hevra kadhisha*—the burial societies that are often in haredi hands and manage funeral processions. At strictly Orthodox funerals, women mourners are expected to stand aside from the graveside ceremony, but now it has become acceptable at most funerals for women to join the main crowd and even chant aloud the mourning kaddish prayer. But clearly the hand of coexistence has not been extended by individual haredi extremists. Some appear to be influenced by the tactics of the right-wing gangs that damage Arab property in reprisal—or as they call it a "price tag"—for setbacks in achieving their political goals. The extremist haredim have taken to defacing public monuments such as Yad Vashem and historic objects. In the spring of 2012, they vandalized the beautiful mosaic floor of a recently discovered synagogue from the Byzantine period as retribution for the alleged desecration of ancient Jewish graves by the government's department of antiquities.

Rational optimists imbued with the secular Zionist tradition believe that a pluralistic society will develop over time and that the coercive nature of the haredi community will weaken if more haredim obtain a less restrictive education that emphasizes core subjects of use in the modern world and if they serve in the army and join the labor force. Some optimists in Israel's secular camp foresee additional haredi compromises, including allowing more public transport on the Sabbath.

The late Dr. Judith Elizur, who had hoped to write a portion of this book, remained an optimist to the day of her death. The daughter of a Conservative rabbi, she carried the deep conviction that Jewish law was not a static concept but a living, ever developing way of life. She believed that various modernizing forces and above all the connective power of communications would induce change. Since the birth of Zionism as a product of the European Enlightenment, its strength in promoting Jewish national revival has grown out of the coalition between emancipated Jews emphasizing the humanistic element of Jewish history and culture, and the religious Jews who insisted on the spiritual value of the law itself. She believed that postmodern society would triumph, thanks to the Internet and the ever-increasing reach and complexity of the cell phone.

Earlier and more widely than in any other country, Israelis learned to depend on the cell phone as an element of personal security; even the poorest parents gave the electronic gadgets to their children so they would stay alert and in touch during the waves of terrorist attacks. When Orthodox rabbis became aware that these phones enabled their followers to reach out to a world beyond their control, they decreed that only phones of limited range could be used in haredi schools. There is every indication that this rule has been ignored by both parents and children, who like most Israelis are as addicted to their smartphones as to their television. The haredi leadership first attempted to prevent its flock from watching TV, and then to limit viewing to broadcasts with "the right message." This too was widely ignored. As for the Internet, a haredi prohibition is still nominally in force, but there are cracks in the wall. Underground websites and even films by haredi women on domestic subjects (ostensibly to be watched only by other women) are being produced without a rabbinical stamp of approval.

It may be significant that haredim living in New York are probably even more worried than their Israeli brethren by the effect of modern technology on their separatist way of life. In May 2012, sixty thousand worried haredim rallied at Citi Field to protest the threat to Jewish tradition by the Internet. In Jerusalem the cellular telephone is used by most young people and regarded as a serious threat by the haredi leadership. In New York, where most haredim hold jobs or run their own businesses, the Internet has become an indispensable tool of commerce but is nevertheless regarded as a dangerous element of modernization. Faced with this dilemma, speakers at the New York rally concentrated on its possibilities for sexual exploration and exhibitionism and suggested that Internet connections be limited to the workplace and banned from the home, where it is more accessible to the younger generation. The New York assembly indicated that the hopes of the late Dr. Elizur would be fulfilled over time and advances in communications technology would weaken haredi influence.

Even the most obscurantist rabbis have been forced to realize that in the modern world it is no longer possible to enforce the literal meaning of all biblical commands. Thus, in view of what is now known about the predisposition toward homosexuality, it would be impossible to follow the explicit order of execution of homosexuals in the book of Leviticus. The founders of modern Israel believed in change. Millions of Arabs tapped into social networks to throw off dictatorships and create an Arab Spring. Were it not for the reports through smartphones and other cellular telephones, the oppressive Assad regime would have probably been more successful in imposing censorship and the world would have probably known much less, if at all, about the bloody fratricide in Syria. As a scholar of communications, Dr. Elizur trusted the power of the word and believed that modern man is influenced not only by the words of his religious teachers and political leaders from on high, but also by what he absorbs through the many and varied outlets of modern media, including the new horizontal social networks of his peers.

Another factor weakening the haredi leadership is the struggle of control over the government's budget. What many in Israel called "the revolt of the Middle Class"—the mass demonstrations in the last part of 2011—was not a specifically anti-haredi movement. It called simply for social justice, but by demanding more aid to the young population whose constructive role in Israeli society had been undermined by the high cost of living and especially housing, the demonstrators in fact demanded a different allocation of the country's resources. Young couples who serve in the army and on whose work and talents the welfare of Israel depends deserve a larger share of the country's wealth. Students arrive at university after three or more years of military service and, unlike yeshiva students, have to pay high tuition fees. They also receive no living allowance, unlike yeshiva students, and most must work while studying. While the haredim obtain state support to house their large families, young secular families have until now been eligible for only scant government assistance to buy an apartment.

Given such disparities in government aid, the conflict between the haredim and the secular political parties is far less concerned with the nature of Zionism than the size of the allocations within the government's budget. The haredim will remain in the government as long as they are convinced that they will not obtain larger benefits in an alternative government, but there now is another dimension. In recent years, they have cheered on Netanyahu's nationalist policies and not just hung on to his purse strings. Their suspicion of all Arabs and their fear of a two-state solution has further secured the budgetary ties linking the ultra-Orthodox parties with Netanyahu and his nationalist supporters.

While there are many persons of goodwill, the conflict is really not about ideology but money. Who deserves more government aid for housing—those who can repay it or those who are so burdened by children and who have so little prospect of employment? The haredim are unable to feed themselves and need the secular taxpayers, whom they despise for driving on the Sabbath and for ignoring strict kashrut, yet who are essential to the nation's defense against Palestinians who want to drive all Jews into the sea, secular and religious alike. A compromise is possible, but only if more haredim work and serve in the army. It is not necessary to subsidize as many as one hundred thousand yeshiva students to preserve traditional Jewish culture. Compromise is not an agreement in which one side always asks for more and expects to receive additional government assistance. There are many haredim who deep in their hearts long for a different life, like the pseudonymous Yanky. But many more such Yankys must be ready to dare to warn their rabbis that without a compromise there will be no Jewish life in the historic homeland, neither haredi nor secular.

Some battles waged in Israel's war within may appear more menacing to an outsider than they really are. One is the place of women in Israeli society. Extreme cases of brutality against women, gender separation in buses, and the refusal of some army units to schedule concerts by women singers are truly inexcusable and reminiscent of Jim Crow segregation in the United States. But repellent as they are, they constitute only a small part of Israeli life.

A tourist who uses all available means of public transportation—rail, bus, and taxi—is unlikely to find herself riding one of the few Mehadrin buses where women must board from the back. A Jerusalemite who recently attended a concert of operatic arias presented by five prominent divas was surprised to notice the large proportion of men in the audience with skullcaps and beards. Far more discriminatory, and hence harder to dislodge, is a more traditional reality that attempts to ground itself with Talmudic or even biblical legitimacy. The rule of rabbinical courts in matters of personal status, and above all marriage and divorce; the separation of boys and girls in some schools; the fact that women can vote but there is no guarantee that women members of the Knesset may represent them—all are battles against intolerance and obscurantism.

But there are also welcome signs that change is possible. With more haredim seeking jobs, they will not only earn money but make friends outside their restrictive community. They will realize that they have much to learn apart from the Talmud. They will also learn that service in the army, while it involves hardships and dangers, has its compensations and can provide satisfactions in their weakening of their social isolation. Above all, military service in Israel is one of the great wellsprings of individual self-confidence. No conscript can avoid engaging his own officers in an explanation of his or her orders—and then being told to work out the problem alone or with his comrades. Such experience is not likely to bind a young person to rigid rabbinical rules.

Many Israelis and Jews abroad often ask themselves the simple questions: When did the War Within begin? When did it intensify and why? A serious, candid introspection on both sides of the conflict will trace its roots to the arrival from Eastern Europe in the mid-nineteenth century of thousands of pious, ultra-Orthodox Jews escaping the emancipation that affected the

Jewish masses. At the beginning, when they were an absolute majority of Jews, the haredim had the upper hand. But in the 1930s, hundreds of thousands of secular Jews settled in Palestine in flight from European anti-Semitism. The clash between the new arrivals and the Orthodox pioneers of the Holy Land has continued over "the proper way of life" and gathered momentum. One Israeli writer remembers as a child a grim-faced assembly every Friday evening at twilight on a deserted street near his home. Hundreds of bearded men in black coats and broad black hats gathered in front of a local beauty parlor that did not send home its last women clients long enough before the arrival of the Sabbath. There was no violence, but the angry shouting and curses were enough to send waves of fright through the neighborhood.

As long as such extremists represented only a small minority of the population, they could be overlooked or at least somehow tolerated as a kind of local eccentricity. But their growing numbers and growing dependence on government aid for housing and welfare to compensate for the gradual decline of contributions from abroad have made untenable the relations between Israel's working majority and the minority with its self-imposed poverty. While there are no indications of a possible agreement with haredi leadership, there are more and more indications that individual haredim are prepared to take their destiny into their own hands.

There are already some signs of the weakening of haredi social isolation. Yeshiva students in their broad-brimmed hats and black suits mingle with the largely secular visitors to Jerusalem's Biblical Zoo, the Yad Vashem Holocaust Museum, the Diaspora Museum in Tel Aviv, as well as the museums commemorating the underground Jewish armies formed before independence. Haredi youth can also be spotted roaming in less commendable places, for example, almost-deserted Jerusalem streets late at night, when they often can be seen smoking or even drinking vodka in youthful rebellion against the stringent discipline of their schools. A rising minority is expressing its objections in more constructive ways. Estimates are necessarily imprecise, but between 10 and 20 percent of all yeshiva students drop out to support their families.

But no less important are the indications of a break in the ban on core studies in haredi schools and the success of schools like Magen Avot (Shield of Our Fathers) in Beit Shemesh, where haredi students are increasingly following a standard academic curriculum. The numbers are still relatively small—about three thousand in the year 2011—but it is the rapid rate of increase in recent years that is remarkable. If this trend gathers force, then the problem will begin to resolve itself and Israel will fulfill Herzl's Zionist vision—not of a Jewish state but a state for Jews, where all religions, including the Jewish religion, can be practiced freely and unencumbered by dogma. This of course is too easy a conclusion; other forceful factors, political, psychological, and sociological, weigh in the balance, and it is too early to say which way it will swing.

And yet Israel's war within has been fed by too much money and not ideology, and this has led to a kind of dictatorial extremism that is alien to Jewish tradition: too many yeshiva students without enough excellence of thought and argument; too many nonworkers, which destroyed the traditional goal of *torah umelacaha*—study and creativity; too many restrictions on women whose work feeds too many of the men who only study; too much personal dependence on the efforts of others—those who defend Israel, those who produce the goods that feed the excess population of scholars. Too much money is diverted to the large cohort that maintains kashrut and others who live off religion, including the duplication of rabbis for the various communities and rabbinical courts. Perhaps even more disturbing than the money spent on the enforcement of a one-sided religious autocracy is the lack of tolerance of other, somewhat different ways of serving God in Israel. While the state formally tolerates all religions and allows all believers to practice as they choose, it denies this right to Jews who have to go abroad for a wedding ceremony recognized by Israeli courts.

Social conflicts like this rarely if ever end in signed agreements, but it is clear that unless the quarrels between religious and secular extremes are not resolved in a spirit of tolerance, the Jewish foundations of the Israeli state will crumble and the state itself risks fragmentation. However far-fetched it may seem, such a fragmented land could revert to a single Palestinian state with an Arab majority, and the haredi extremists would attain their goal of the end of Zionism, but also of their own way of life in the Holy Land, for such an Arab-dominated polity would surely lead to their expulsion, or worse. For this threat to recede, several policies must be agreed upon by all factions. First and foremost, all Israeli Jews must serve in the nation's armed forces for as long as the law requires. Those who are unwilling to defend their homeland have no moral claim to live in it. As a corollary, those who complete military service should receive a standard stipend to aid in continuing their studies, whether academic or religious. The young must also be prepared for the modern world, and the curriculum of every Israeli school therefore should include the core subjects of English, mathematics, and history. And finally, when they marry, all couples should be able to do so through an authorized religious functionary of their choice. These principles are clear enough and remain essential if Israel is to maintain its place among the nations of the modern world. Working out details is never easy, but Jews have a historical inheritance of biblical analysis and Talmudic debate that makes them uniquely qualified for such a task. No one would benefit more than the Jewish nation if, instead of mutual intolerance and vilification, these talents were turned toward making peace instead of continuing to wage the War Within.

Selected Bibliography

Arian, Asher. 1980. *The Elections in Israel*. Jerusalem Academic Press (English).

Ben-Yehuda, Nachman. 2010. *Theocratic Democracy: The Social Construction of Religious and Secular Extremism*. New York: Oxford University Press (English).

Caplan, Kimmy, and Emmanuel Sivan, editors. 2003. *Israeli Haredim-Integration without Assimilation*. Jerusalem: Van Leer Institute (Hebrew).

Davis, Moshe, editor. 1980. *Zionism in Transition*. New York: Herzl Press (English).

Elizur, Yuval. 2010. *The Assault on Secular Israel*. Jerusalem: Carmel (Hebrew).

Elizur, Yuval, and Salpeter, Eliahu. 1973. *Who Rules Israel?* New York: Harper and Row (English).

Elon, Amos. 2004. *The Pity of It All*. London: Penguin Books (English).

Friedman, Menahem. 2001. *Society in Legitimacy Crisis*. Jerusalem: Bialik Institute (Hebrew).

Gonen, Amiram. 2000. *From Yeshiva to Work*. Jerusalem: Floersheimer Institute for Policy Studies (English).

Heilman, Samuel. 1992. *Defenders of the Faith—Inside Ultra Orthodox Jewry*. New York: Schocken Books (English).

Horowitz, David. 1975. *In the Heart of Events.* Ramat-Gan: Masada (Hebrew).

Ilan, Shahar. 2003. *Haredim Ltd.* Jerusalem: Keter (Hebrew).

Leshem, Elazar, and Judith T. Shuval. 1998. *Immigration to Israel—Sociological Perspectives.* Rutgers University Press, New Brunswick, NJ.

Medzini, Meron. 2008. *Golda.* Tel Aviv: Yediot Acharonot Books and Chemed Books (Hebrew).

Pearl, Moshe. 2003. *While We Were Watching.* Jerusalem: Keter (Hebrew).

Sharett, Moshe. 1978. *Personal Diary* (eight volumes). Tel-Aviv: Ma'ariv (Hebrew).

Shilav, Yosseph. 1998. *Ultra Orthodoxy in Urban Governance.* Jerusalem: Floersheimer Institute for Policy Studies (English).

Stern, Yedidiah Z. 2003. *Facing Painful Choices—Law and Halacha in Israeli Society.* Jerusalem: Israel Democracy Institute (English).

INDEX